With love and
Light –
    In Spirit –
        Leslie

"Spirit is the essence of our being—love."
Gerald Jampolsky, M.D.; and **Diane V. Cirincione, Ph.D.**

"Spirit makes you succeed when everything else fails.
(I have some jokes in my files that could have used some Spirit.)"
Bob Hope

"I remember that Jesus told Nicodemus that Spirit was like the wind,
in that we can't see it but can see its effects, which are profound.
I see the word representing the essence of a being or a thing,
whether it be God, another person, myself, evil, or goodness.
To me, the closest synonym is *soul*."
Jimmy Carter

"The soul is the center of our being.
It is home to our goodness, our love,
our consciousness, and our compassion.
I believe Spirit is how we communicate these feelings.
Spirit is what connects us to God and to each other."
Roma Downey

"Spirit is the essence and consciousness
of one's soul—dark and enlightened.
Both extremes are vital and should be left to flourish unrestricted.
For in that journey discoveries are made."
Andy Garcia

WHAT IS SPIRIT?

MESSAGES FROM THE HEART

LEXIE BROCKWAY POTAMKIN

WITH ART by PETER MAX

HAY HOUSE, INC.
Carlsbad, California • Sydney, Australia

Published and distributed in the United States by:
Hay House, Inc., P.O. Box 5100, Carlsbad, CA 92018-5100 • (800) 654-5126 • (800) 650-5115 (fax)

Editorial: Jill Kramer and Chris Watsky • Art Direction: *Christy Salinas* • *Design:* Bachner + Co.

Library of Congress Cataloging-in-Publication Data

What is spirit :   messages from the heart / [compiled by] Lexie
   Brockway Potamkin ;   artwork by Peter Max.
         p.   cm.
      ISBN 1-56170-675-2 (hardcover)
      1. Spirit Quotations, maxims, etc.   I. Potamkin, Lexie Brockway.
   BD423.W48   1999
   128'.1–dc21
                                                                   99-23614
                                                                   CIP

                          ISBN 1-56170-675-2

                    02 01 00 99   4 3 2 1
                    First Printing, October 1999

                 Printed by Palace Press Hong Kong

*Dedicated to Mickey, who taught me that it is more
important to be loving than to be right.*

Acknowledgments

"Your vision will become clear only when you can look into your own heart."
Carl Jung

This book would not have been possible without the love and support of my wonderful friends and family. Their unconditional love is one of my greatest blessings.

My heartfelt thanks to Lori Blackman; Michele Blickman; Alvin and Judy Block; Marco Borges; Larry Brockway; Laura Brockway; Myrna Brind; Dollie Cole; Elliott Curson; Christine Davies; Robert Doornick; Traci Fisher; Marc Ganzi; Melissa Ganzi; Baby Grant; Gail Gross; Anatoly Ivanov; Jerry Jampolsky and Diane Cirincione; Liz Kalogris; Arlan Kardon; Betty Kibler; Debbie Mattos; Sharon McNamara; Eddie Micone; Robert Potamkin; Toby Schmidt Schachman; Lonna Shuttlesworth; Millinda Sinnreich; Ted Solomon; Vada Stanley; Randy Swartz; Dorothy and Hal Thau; Petrina Wells; and Nessie and Ralph Yara, whose time, work, and ideas were the foundation of this book.

Thank you to Daniel Levin at Hay House for your support and nurturing of this project; and to Laura Norman for connecting me to Daniel. Thank you to Christy Salinas and Jill Kramer for your thoughtful suggestions and comments. Thank you to Peter Max whose colorful artwork makes the inspirational quotes and stories come alive. A special thank you to Laurie Sue Brockway, my friend and colleague.

Without her steadfast support, this book would never have been completed.

I am deeply grateful to all the many people throughout the world who have shared with me their thoughts about Spirit. Their contributions have been invaluable.

Special thanks to: Gregg R. Anderson, Nick Ault, Robert Baldwin, Michelle S.K. Ball, Ellen Barr, Olga Berencen, Debbie Berk, Jayne Bernsten, Kathy Bernsten, Karen Jacobson Bruno, Yolanda Cecilia, Richard J. Cohen, Michael Cohn, Katherine L. Cone, Margit Corner, Lois A. Edwards, Ali W. Ejjam, Pamela D. Fisher, Amy Thau Friedman, Jane Scacetti Fumo, Vince Fumo, Donna Laurent Gabler, Elizabeth Ganzi, Susan Lee Gilbert, Lisa Hammond, Joe Henry, Trip Huxley, Anatoly Ivanov, Carole L. Johnson, Evan Kardon, Harisen Kardon, Nakia Langston, Soto Keouth, Daniel Hampton Kibler, William L. Kirt, Joann Klynman, Andreas Kurz, Mary Lilly, Lexie Luce, Judith Marinoff, Brittany McNamara, Justin McNamara, Lynn Miller, Robert Muller, Gayatri Naraine, Dorothy Nassar, Helene B. Newman, Russ Oasis, Katie Oberwager, Susan Mathes Oberwager, Washburn Oberwager, Sharon R. Opel, David Paskin, Meyer Potamkin, Nathaniel Potamkin, Vivian Orleans Potamkin, Katherine Preston, Martin W. Reddan III, Stephanie Richman, Andrew Schlessinger, Sally M. Seligman, Donna Serpe, Alan Sirkin, Alicia Sirkin, Rose C. Smith, Tina Spitzer, Connie Stern, Jerome H. Stern, Iliana Kloesmeyer Strauss, Shan Stuart, Joanne K. Swanson, Randy Swartz, Paul Taylor, Tony Tognucci, Frederick Warhanek, Edward L. Wolf, and Jaelyn Wolf.

Lexie Brockway Potamkin

CONTENTS

INTRODUCTION

"Do not wait for leaders; do it alone, person to person."
Mother Teresa

As we speed to a new millennium, everybody is busy—busy with work, busy with family, crazy busy just trying to get through daily life. Many of the people who shared their hearts and souls on these pages fall into that category—they are busy people. Some of them are famous for what they do; others quietly nurture their trade without public recognition. They come from different walks of life and hail from different cities and countries. They all have life stories, and together make up a melting pot of people, most of whom have never met one another. Yet they all have one very special thing in common: the word *Spirit* means something to them. It meant enough for them to answer these questions. And in that small gesture, we see a much larger picture unfolding—Spirit is a common bond between us all.

In today's fast-paced society, it meant a lot that so many busy people, often with complex lives, took the time to respond to two questionnaires. One form asked them to describe "What is Spirit?" and the other issued a second difficult challenge: to define themselves so that a brief biographical sketch could be written for the readers to understand the respondents' backgrounds. Some generously gave their time to be interviewed, graciously opening their hearts and sharing their lives.

People dove deep within for an answer and found that along the way, the process opened them to even more of what Spirit means to them.

"I must confess, it was a challenge to define what Spirit means to me," wrote Joan Blackman, a former bank executive. "I went through several stages of thought while trying to put into words what is so personal, yet shared by every being. Just when I thought I might have an understanding, I would look a little deeper and peel off another layer, finding yet another interpretation. For a while, I had a nagging feeling that I *had* to find meaning—for myself."

Even those who you might think would have it "figured out" took the time to search within themselves for the answer that most represented their feelings on the topic.

Richard Bach, author of spiritual classics such as *Jonathan Livingston Seagull* and *Illusions,* said he didn't dare try to describe this ineffable force. "Thanks for the honor of your request," he offered warmly. "When I can define Spirit in words, I shall have become so advanced as to never need words."

"It seems like a simple topic, but for me it's not simple," wrote Gerard Schwarz, music director of the Seattle Symphony. "That's probably why you are doing a book on it."

"Spirit, in its essence, is challenging to capture and define," wrote Robert White, Aspen-based CEO of an international corporate training company who is co-author of *One World, One People* and credited with founding the modern personal growth movement. "Ultimately, perhaps it is the only possession of real, lasting value."

That idea resonated with many people: Spirit is hard to define. It's valuable. It's always there. It's not a material thing. It is the source of something bigger than we are. These are some of the concepts people played with while trying to answer.

A theme that came up repeatedly is that Spirit equals love, and love equals Spirit. As world-renowned author Gerald Jampolsky, M.D.; and his wife/partner, Diane Cirincione, Ph.D., stated: "Spirit is the essence of our being—love." These two have traveled to 45 countries to serve in the name of love. Jerry is the author of *Love Is Letting Go of Fear* and many other books, as well as founder of the Attitudinal Healing Center; Diane has written *Sounds of the Morning Sun*. They have seen the way love can heal and uplift the Spirit, and they make no distinction between the two.

Reading through all these marvelous responses prompted me to write my own answer to the question, "What is Spirit?" I found myself just as amazed as everyone else that there are so many layers to explore, so many petals to be opened.

Although the responses herein are nondenominational and interfaith in nature, I realized that I, like many people, began my experience of Spirit through certain religious teachings that I have embraced in my life and in my heart. For example, when I first began to explore what Spirit meant to me, I thought of the Holy Spirit, which is available to everyone, no matter what religion. Christ spoke often about the Holy Spirit, saying that it's available to anyone who asks. That's why, in my spiritual practice, I am so drawn to the pure nature of the teachings of Christ. He emphasized unconditional love for others, and for self. He spoke about love, forgiveness, understanding, empathy, tolerance, and the gift of the Holy Spirit. Spirit keeps me focused on love and teaches me that the greatest of all things is love.

And, I realized, Spirit is pure, unconditional love. Peaceful and free, it is available to anyone, anytime, anywhere. Tapping into this essence is, I believe, a choice we make, and *can make,* at any moment, because each and every one of us is free to choose love.

Love is the highest state of being, and from that vantage point, many of us have experiences with "Spirit in action" through the lives and contributions of people who embody Spirit. When I began to read the responses from people who very specifically singled out the Spirit they observed in another, I realized that for many people, that's where it all begins. We are touched, moved, or inspired by someone, and we can't figure out what it is about them that stirs something in us. Then the light bulb goes off: *Aha—that's what Spirit looks like!* Spirit at work could be a child at play. Spirit is the child in all of us, the sense of wonder, the joy. And at the same time, Spirit is the common source of who we all are. And as Lao-Tzu, founder of Taoism, said, "When you realize where you come from, you naturally become tolerant, amused, kindhearted as a grandmother, dignified as a king."

Interviewing people I had never met before, yet feeling a very meaningful and deep connection with them, was "Spirit" connecting our souls. Meditating quickly with the Tibetan monks and then "experiencing" their chanting was awesome. It was Spirit in motion. And in that silence, that calm of meditation, I was illuminated. It is a silence in which the Spirit of God can enter us, heal us, and change our lives forever.

Spirit is my two poodles and their unconditional love. Spirit is my father's love guiding me through every day of my life. Spirit is my connection to truth. It's music, it's nature, it's a quiet night at home, it's… well, every time I thought about it, another idea would evolve. It became clearer and clearer that Spirit is a fluid, flowing, moving energy. The more we ask the question, the deeper we get into the question—only to find that there simply is no one answer.

As I continued to ask myself, *What is Spirit?* and to read other people's responses, a new world opened up. I felt uplifted and peaceful—more connected to people, places, life. I felt privy to the truth that there is one huge, gigantic, unfathomable source that is Spirit, and that there are millions of little pathways that lead us to it.

The late Dr. Lee Salk, a famous child psychologist, was a longtime friend. Lee believed that the demise of the family is the demise of society. He encouraged me with his beliefs about the Spirit of family. He told me that the most powerful motivation to live comes from family and the knowledge of being loved, wanted, and needed. One day at his home, I was inspired to ask his brother, Dr. Jonas Salk, for his response to the question, "What is Spirit?" At the time I was frustrated over my work in the human rights field, and he told me not to be discouraged. "Spirit is evolution, and we are an evolving species," said this man who changed the course of history when he discovered the vaccine for polio. I was so awed by the consciousness in his answer. It gave me hope. Perhaps not everyone is interested in thinking about Spirit today, but maybe they will next month, or next year, or sometime in the course of a lifetime, because according to Jonas, we are evolving as a species.

When I told my friend Peter Max about this book, he asked, "How can I help?" As a man of Spirit and one who has long tread the path of spiritual growth, he wanted to be supportive. That, again, is Spirit at work! It is Spirit who brings you the right insights at the right time, brings you together with all those you are meant to meet on your path, and helps you make things happen, all at the appropriate time.

As the question of what Spirit is filtered into my counseling practice, I began to see how cathartic it was for people to look deeply into that question. I saw the question take many individuals back to their core belief system. As a therapist, it wasn't my job to tell them what to believe, but to facilitate their process of uncovering their own truth; tapping into that truth accelerates personal growth. One of the reasons I was so excited about doing this book is that it has that same wonderful, therapeutic effect on people. It helps people assess their reality and make choices about how they want their experiences to be. It helps people stay connected to themselves and their source. *I believe that discovering Spirit reminds us of who we are!*

When you pick up this book, you can turn to any page and find the very thing that will help in the next day—or next moment—of your journey. But before you begin, take a moment to answer the question for yourself: *What is Spirit?*

Use the next page to jot down your thoughts. When you are finished reading, challenge yourself to revisit the question with new spiritual eyes. In the space provided at the end of the book, write another definition. You may find that as you follow the path of Spirit, you will be shown a new aspect, a new possibility. Perhaps we need to begin each day by asking, "If I die, what will I be remembered for?" Then we can begin our daily journey by being the person we truly want to be and living in Spirit. As my dad always said, be careful and thoughtful how you live. You may be the only Bible some people will ever read.

*Before you read on, take a moment to look into your own
heart and soul, and answer the question . . .*

WHAT IS SPIRIT?

Spirit Quotes
And Inspirational Tales*

"Spirit, for me, has almost nothing to do with 'spirituality.' It is simply energy—positive energy and love. The simplest, most humble being can be filled with more Spirit than a lifelong meditator."

Patricia Aburdene, bestselling co-author of *Megatrends for Women*

"Spirit is something that is released once you've popped the cork."

Dwight W. Arundale, celebrated artist

"Spirit is distilled pure love, in and out of eyes, from voices into ears, through every touch and every move, combining in a whiff of ambrosia; it is alive in every being."

Lynne Arundale, writer

*The short quotes about Spirit are in each person's own words. The longer inspirational tales are written about a particular individual by author Lexie Brockway Potamkin. All material in quotations has been edited by the author.

Peter Max "Heart, Version I, # 4" 1995, 20˝ x 16˝, acrylic on canvas

"Spirit makes you succeed when everything else fails.
(I have some jokes in my files
that could have used some spirit)"

Bob Hope

"Spirit is the innate force that drives a person to pursue endeavors positively and enthusiastically, and to work tirelessly and creatively to achieve objectives—be they professional, personal, or for the good of the community."

Sheryl L. Auerbach, senior law firm partner

"My spiritual odyssey began in 1961 and led me from a jet-set life, to the West, to the East, and finally to the knowledge that what I wanted most was to devote my life to the study of Buddhist teachings and to become a Buddhist nun. To do this, I returned to the source, India.

"I arrived at a special school set up to teach Western languages to young incarnate Tibetan Lamas. Situated on a mountain in Northern India was this monastic school and a nunnery about a mile away. In these two teaching centers, I found what I had been searching for—the teachings, a peaceful place to live, and the means to being useful. I also met a man who would, 20 years later, become my husband.

"Impermanence is the core teaching of the Buddha, so it wasn't long before I was forced to leave, and return my vows. The year 1980 found me in London; one phone call changed my life forever. A Tibetan Tulku or Incarnate Lama whom I met 20 years earlier telephoned, and after identifying himself, asked if I would like to have dinner. We were married a year later in New York. I have no doubt that 'Big Hand' was/is there and that my task in this life is to care for my Tulku husband, as he does me."

Jane Werner Aye, former Tibetan Buddhist nun

LAURA BROCKWAY

When I think of Spirit, two people come to mind: my mother, Laura Brockway, and my grandmother, Ethel Foster. That is why this first inspirational tale I am sharing with you is about my own family. Spirit—my grandmother had it; my mother still does. In these two powerfully spiritual women, I find the roots of my own understanding about what Spirit really is: It is an essence we can often see best when we observe and experience it in those we admire. How they face adversity and triumph, and in doing so, pass a gift of courage and understanding to those around them.

My grandmother was born and raised in Michigan. At the tender age of 17, she met and fell in love with my grandfather. He was from Idaho, so she packed up her entire life, said good-bye to her family and friends, and moved across the country to settle with him in his home state. The train ride from Idaho to Michigan was quite a long haul in those days, and hard on the pocketbook, so she did not see her family much. Instead, she had a family of her own and raised them with Spirit. She lived to see many grandchildren and great-grandchildren grow into wonderful beings. She lived a simple life, sometimes a rugged one, yet she lived it rich in Spirit. She was loving, giving of herself, and faithful to those she loved. I always felt that it took great Spirit—and faith in Spirit—to leave her family, her friends, and the life she knew to move to a place she had never even seen to be with the man she loved. It took Spirit to make it work and keep it working. In my life, she was the role model and pioneer of Spirit in my family.

She passed her great essence along to my wonderful mother, Laura, who, after four major open-heart surgeries, still completely trusts in Spirit. My mother knows Spirit so intimately that she has maintained a strong and positive attitude throughout. Not only has she survived, but she has thrived—and she has amazed every physician who cared for her. Time and again she has bounced back from all she's been through. She gets me through every crisis in her life by saying: "God and the angels are with me, and my family is the wind beneath my wings."

My mother lives in a constant state of grace, embracing Spirit and all of life with her warm, cheery, positive personality. "I just know everything's going to be all right, and I'm never afraid," she says. "I think it's faith. I have this feeling that everything is okay. I don't know of anything to pinpoint it. It is just a lot of faith. You face a lot of things in your life that, without faith… I don't know how you'd get through it."

Even in the face of her greatest losses in life—the death of my dad, and a brother I never knew who died of streptococcus when he was just a year old—she gathered strength and courage. "You have to go on," she says. "You can always look around and see someone worse off than you are. You cannot dwell on it."

What is Spirit? "It's inside you; it's what keeps you going," my mother says. "It gives you happiness. Without Spirit, you would hardly exist. It is the light of our life, the faith of our life. It is purity of thought. It is the very inner being of yourself—the inner world of thought, feeling, love, light, beauty. It is the goodness that shines through as love for all others, a spiritual kindness, a gentleness, the inner being of joy and happiness. Without Spirit, we would not have faith. It is everything that guides us."

My mother's philosophy is that every little prayer helps. She has been known to get her doctors to pray with her before surgery—but, she says, "Do not wait until you are facing a medical emergency to start praying. Many people suddenly start when there is a crisis. There has to be something important in your life that keeps you connected—Spirit is what does that."

The divine spark in my mother, and hers before her, provided the world view with which I was raised. And I am fortunate that both my grandmother and my mother have passed along to me their beautiful connection to the expression of Spirit!

max 12.31.94

Peter Max "Day Dream, Version 1, #5" 1996, 30" x 40", acrylic on canvas

"Spirit is the breath of God,
a universal energy that, once created,
can never be destroyed"

Wynonna Judd

"What is Spirit? When one becomes a child of God through a personal relationship with the crucified, risen, living, and coming-again Son of God, then *Spirit* truly takes on significance. Beginning at that point, one's words, attitudes, motivations, actions, desires, goals, and responses to disappointments and victories in life, as well as relationships with people, are all tempered and molded by a desire to bring glory to God…"

Ruth Babbitt, faculty advisor to the National Honor Society

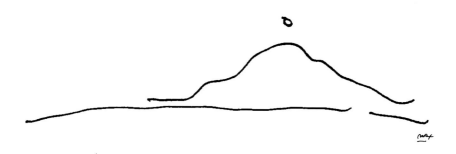

"Spirit is eternal—it has always existed; Spirit is truth, for it exists on every level and in any context. Because of this, Spirit and truth may be thought of as one and the same. Spirit is, most of all, *being*…"

Peter Baterna, acupuncturist, massage therapist, portfolio manager

"Spirit is when your brain and your heart become one. When presented with a visual scene or experience, everything that you've learned in your brain stirs a powerful, uplifting emotion within your heart."

Cheryl A. Beck, business development manager for a news radio station

"I had no Spirit while facing the cruelty and inhumanity of Castro's prison. Today, Spirit is being born again with the chance to start over again, making a new life and being useful."

Ramberto Berencen, former Cuban political prisoner, now 78

Richard Block

In 1978, Richard Block (co-founder of H&R Block), was diagnosed with lung cancer and told that he had three months to live. It was an awakening that led him on the journey of a lifetime—from an intimate and painful closeness to death, to emerging completely alive and reaching out to help others.

Before his diagnosis, Richard Block was living a typical Type-A lifestyle—working hard during tax season and playing hard during the down time. He smoked three packs of cigarettes a day, quitting just a year before this diagnosis.

Cancer completely shifted his life. "All of a sudden I realized that there are a lot of other things much more important," he recalls. "Spirit sure had something to do with it. I've always been fairly spiritual, but cancer made me realize that the values in life were not what I always thought they were."

Doctors gave him two paths: a chance for life, or certain death. The doctor who offered him life literally made him an offer he could not refuse. "First, I was told that I was terminal and there was nothing I could do," Richard Block says. "I went to another doctor and his statement was, 'Dick, you're a very sick boy, and we are going to make you a lot sicker, but we are going to cure you... so you will be working.' I said, 'If you do, I will.' He made me a lot sicker, but he cured me. And ever since then, my wife and I have devoted our lives to helping others."

In 1982, he sold his interest in H&R Block and began to devote his efforts to cancer research. "It is a very narrow goal. The next person who gets cancer has the best chance of beating it. It is less important to find a cure for cancer or to eliminate the cause of cancer, because we do not know anything about those things. But we do know something about treatments for cancer. So we are trying to help people who have it get a better chance of beating it."

Richard Block and his wife, Annette, founded an array of free services for cancer patients. The Cancer Hotline in Kansas City, a volunteer organization, has handled more than 60,000 calls from newly diagnosed cancer patients since 1980. They instituted the now-standard procedure of getting a second opinion when founding the R.A. Block Cancer Management Center at the University of Missouri. From 1980 to 1995, the multi disciplinary second-opinion panel was staffed by over 100 physicians who donated their time. The center was closed only after the concept mainstreamed, and in 1988 the Blocks dedicated the grounds of the R.A. Block Cancer Support Center as a support and education facility. The couple has written several books.

You will not hear him speak of the more esoteric nature of his personal experience with cancer and the path that it put him on, yet it is clear that he approaches this work with great enthusiasm.

"My parents used to say that once you have three meals a day, you'd better do something for somebody else," Richard Block says. "Everything we do is free. My wife and I pay for everything."

He says that his wife of 52 years believes that he was given the experiences and resources to be able to help other cancer patients increase their chances of survival. Some would say that this is Spirit at work. "My wife often tells me that this is my mission," he says.

What is Spirit? "Spirit is the drive or will to excel."

"The Human Spirit is the everlasting gift that God has given all of us. I believe it is the part of us that He filled with compassion, joy, peace, gentility, and kindness; I believe He did this with the intention that we call upon it when interacting with all living creatures."

Joan Blackman, happily married to a corporate lawyer

"Spirit is a gift from God. It is uniquely different in every one of us. We are all born in the image and likeness of God. But it is that gift that makes us different from anyone else. Spirit is strength, love, and wisdom, and it keeps us whole as we travel through life.

"Without even realizing it, we give it to others through ourselves every day. And when the Maker calls and our body is no longer a part of this world, the Spirit of what we have given to others remains. The body dies, but our Spirit never does. It's a gift, and it remains with everyone you have touched in your lifetime."

Jerry Blavat, TV/radio entertainer credited with creating the oldies nostalgia-craze in 1962

"I believe that Spirit is the unique and ever-present Voice that resides in the center of us, whether it be still and small or resounding and clear; whether we wish to not hear and heed it, or wish to welcome its rightness and be guided by it. The Voice is God's personal message to each of us, our guidebook for daily living, and our road map for life."

Jimmer Bolden, lease administrator for video stores; professional vocalist

JIMMY CARTER

As 39th President of the United States, Jimmy Carter dedicated himself to restoring the tenet of compassion to government. He was architect of the 1979 Camp David Accords, in which he brought the nations of Egypt and Israel together in a historic reconciliation. As an elder statesman, he continues his passionate support of human rights and other humanitarian causes through the Atlanta-based Carter Center.

He is a hands-on activist—monitoring human rights issues in third-world countries, reaching out to help exiled Tibetans, traveling around the world to build homes for Habitat for Humanity, even helping his hometown build a community center. He has authored books on many aspects of life—from poetry to aging to his recent *Living Faith*.

"I really wanted to call the book *Faith Is a Verb*, since faith is an active rather than passive experience," says Carter, a devout Christian who shares his thoughtful views on faith and Spirit in his book and in his Sunday Bible-study classes at the Maranatha Baptist Church in his hometown of Plains, Georgia.

For Carter, faith is to be placed not only in God. "I had faith in my mother, first, and then both my parents. Later in my life I had faith in my nation, and I was inspired by patriotism—by a willingness to give my life, if necessary, in a submarine force to protect the interests of my country. When I served as president, I was filled with patriotism.

During a lifetime, we all evolve an element of faith that guides us and inspires us. And I guess the word *inspire* involves an inner spirit."

That inner spirit, if nurtured by our government and amplified around the world, could also be applied to making basic human rights available to all peoples. "There's only one superpower now, and that's the United States," he says. "What we should have, as a nation, is a commitment to the basic principles that make a life admirable: a commitment to justice, to peace, to generosity toward people in need, to treating them with basic human rights. These are the kinds of things that I tried to adopt as globally acknowledged commitments of America when I was president."

Sometimes the spirit of compassion and service is awakened by witnessing the despair of others. To this end, Carter regularly travels to foreign countries. He points out that the Carter Center now has programs in 35 African countries.

"I don't think there is any doubt that if we are shocked out of our lethargy or out of our self-protective cocoon by an awareness of other people's intense suffering, we become motivated by an inner spirit to help alleviate their concerns or problems and share what we have," he says. "When I go and see whole villages suffering from easily controllable diseases, or see children who are not immunized against basic illnesses, or see people starving to death when they have land that could very easily provide them food, that gives me a spirit of service. It's not unpleasant. It's a self-fulfilling ambition that brings me gratification and pleasure."

As he suggests in *Living Faith,* the spirit of love can motivate people to action. He has seen the profound impact of love in places around the world, "even between people who begin by despising each other but find a way to see the image of God in each other's humanity."

He recalls that some of his more extraordinary experiences with Spirit occurred "between" elections on his path to becoming governor of Georgia.

"When I was defeated for governor in 1966, I went on three pioneer mission programs for my church—to Lockhaven, Pennsylvania; to Springfield, Massachusetts; and to the southern part of Atlanta," he says. "I was just carried away with the presence of the Holy Spirit.

"I told Rosalynn that when I went to visit families and talk with them about my own faith, I felt I didn't have any responsibility of my own except just to do the best I could, and that the outcome of the conversations were completely controlled by the Holy Spirit. We had 48 people who accepted Christ as Savior in Lockhaven, and in just a week we started a new church."

What is Spirit? "I remember that Jesus told Nicodemus that Spirit was like the wind, in that we can't see it but can see its effects, which are profound. I see the word representing the essence of a being or a thing, whether it be God, another person, myself, evil, or goodness. To me, the closest synonym is *soul*."

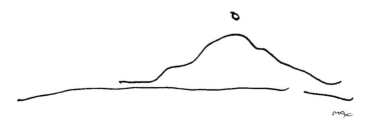

"Spirit is inner peace and awareness; it's what makes us smile for no reason at all. It's the most efficient way to communicate. It's the best song, the brightest sunrise. It's our connection to every other person or thing on Earth. Without Spirit the body breaks down.

"Spirit is the little voice inside that always makes the right decisions. Whether or not you realize and act on them is up to you. In business, I always trust my Spirit even when I don't understand. It's been very good to me so far."

Marco Borges, Miami's foremost fitness expert

"Spirit is the energy that puts passions into play."

Irvin J. Borowsky, chairman of The Liberty Museum in Philadelphia

"I can only take my ordained place as part of Spirit when I am free of fear and resentment; when I am out of self and in full surrender. My level of Spirit-consciousness is inversely proportional to my level of self-consciousness. I must turn at all times and in all circumstances to the Spirit within me."

Jim Bramble, retired lawyer; active member of Alcoholics Anonymous for 34 years

Peter Max "Flag with Heart, Version XIII, #1" 1993, 24″ x 36″, acrylic on canvas

"Spirit {is} like the wind, in that we can't see it
but can see its effects, which are profound"

Jimmy Carter

"Spirit is the embodiment of life. It is with us from birth to death. It defines who and what we are."

Larry Brockway, owner of his own company

"Spirit *is* Alexander, my son, who is a being of light, joy, and loving presence. Alexander came here a tiny bundle of medical challenges, with one leg and the need for many surgeries. Yet from the day he was born, his soul energy filled the neonatal intensive-care unit with a huge, pervading determination to be part of this world. As he healed, grew, and developed, it became clear that he was an embodiment of the Spirit of hope, healing, wisdom, and possibility. I have never met a being so filled with light—Spirit in action!—nor have I ever met anyone as willing as Alexander to show the world that *we are all* God's children, created in the image of the divine, and filled with divinity within! He has taught me that 'perfection' is being who we are and who we are meant to be. And that Spirit is a force far greater than the container God gives us to express it through."

Rev. Laurie Sue Brockway, journalist-turned-interfaith minister, teacher, and author

"Spirit is the ability to face adversity—to come from behind and win with grace."

Amber Brookman, CEO, business supporter of the Welfare-to-Work Program

ROMA DOWNEY

God loves you. No one says it better than Monica, the beautiful and compassionate angel who comes to Earth in order to work as a spiritual social worker for an assortment of troubled, searching, and confused humans on the CBS hit series *Touched by an Angel.*

With her familiar Irish lilt, the Northern Ireland–born actress Roma Downey has become one of the millennium's most meaningful television characters. The Emmy winner and Golden Globe Award nominee speaks to the heart and soul of our search for Spirit by portraying a celestial being in human form who has real emotions, compassion, and a deep desire to heal others by awakening them to the existence of Spirit in their lives.

"I am an angel sent by God," her character admits, coming out of the celestial closet. That proclamation, always followed by a glow of heavenly light behind and above her head, is something we all want to believe. She makes us want to believe in Spirit, in something beyond this day-to-day life, in the idea that we are loved enough that someone—like an angel—has come to give a guiding hand.

Just as Monica, affectionately called "Miss Wings," has steadily developed into a more skillful, focused, and mature angel, it seems that Downey's life in many ways has run on a parallel track, with experiences that have nurtured her growth and her spiritual evolution. She sees spiritual life with the same grace, style, and commitment that her character expresses.

What is Spirit to this actress? "The soul is the center of our being. It is home to our goodness, our love, our consciousness, and our compassion," she says. "I believe Spirit is how we communicate these feelings. Spirit is what connects us to God and to each other."

"I think a person who is truly spiritual is free of all selfishness and just savors the gift of life and love of God. We're born into our Spirit. I don't think we're born and then a Spirit comes in. I think the Spirit is here first and then we come in. It's definitely the power source of life."

John Bruno, martial artist, musician, auto executive, pilot

"What is Spirit *not?*"

Kristi Cadwell, poet, teacher, artist

"*What is Spirit?* I'll probably continue, the rest of my life, to look for the right words to completely and clearly describe something that, the more I think about it, may be impossible to capture with mere words. But let me share this: While love is what makes the world go 'round, Spirit is what makes the ride worthwhile!"

Kevin Carlisle, producer/director/choreographer

"I believe that Spirit is the very essence of a human being. The purest, most honest, and defining aspect of a person is the Spirit of that person. Someone who is of good spirit is gracious, self-satisfied, and, in fact, grateful for all that life presents."

Yolanda Cecilia, volunteer for Guardian Ad Litem, an advocacy group for children

"My Olympic family's gift of skiing in Vermont connected me as a child to the awesome beauty of nature, which sharpened my self-esteem and the intuitive voice that has been my faithful guide in life. When I moved to Telluride in '95, I exchanged the joy of skiing with Rollingbears, a beautiful Lakota-Sioux man, for the wisdom of his culture. He opened up a world to me that few Anglos are aware of, where the Great Spirit miraculously takes care of us without needing to hoard, because we are all part of a living, loving Universe. Giving our unique gift for the greater good of all is the ultimate high.

"In helping to heal our spirits and those of the first Americans, our guides to survival for the 21st century, I have found my gift, my purpose, and my passion. I am now a billionaire in spirit!"

Suzy Chaffee, Olympic champion skier, proponent of women's and amateurs' rights in sports

I believe in God the Father and that His Spirit is intimately and personally involved in our lives. I believe I have seen His Spirit at work in all areas of my life, personal and professional, seeking to draw me and those around me to a closer, loving relationship with Him and each other."

Chayanne, Latin pop singer-turned-movie actor who starred in the film *Dance with Me*

El Puma

For legions of devoted fans, Jose Luis Rodriguez is *it!* He has often been referred to as the Frank Sinatra of Latin music. His signature name is El Puma, meaning "The Cougar." His voice is deliciously smooth, romantic, and inviting; his music has a way of opening the heart and connecting the soul to something greater than itself. It is clear that Spirit comes through him.

El Puma's music is universal in its ability to touch. He is loved, and his music is adored, around the world—from the Americas to Asia and Europe. His many platinum records prove that. Yet he is the first to acknowledge that his great voice and beautiful music are gifts he has been given by God, and that life is impermanent, so he is trying to awaken the Spirit as much as possible. In his personal life, he is very quiet and shy. Yet El Puma, even on an ordinary day, is as soulful as his music suggests.

"We all come from Number One, which is God," El Puma says. "He broke himself into billions of pieces and made us out of them. So we are all extensions of God. We are just temporary beings, temporary inhabitants of this earth. I believe that God has had many different forms, but the best role he has played to date has been Jesus Christ. I give thanks to God for letting me know his mystery. I have been allowed to inhabit this earth in a better form because I have more spirituality."

What is Spirit? "Spirit comes from something greater and returns to something greater," he says. "It is not something that can be taken away or given to you. It is something that's already yours and you can just do with it as you please. Eventually it is going to return to wherever it came from.

"Spirit involves all human beings," he says. "I think Earth is a school. We came to Earth basically to graduate from the school of Spirit to spirituality. From the time we are born, the body starts to degenerate, yet our spirituality increases. We become more aware as time goes on. When we leave, the only thing we take with us is our Spirit. Everything else stays—body, clothes, material things. The only real, real thing that goes with us is our Spirit.

"Spirituality is something that must be sought out by each individual. God does not go looking for anyone," he says. "You have to seek within yourself. Spirit, on the other hand, does not exist in time or space—it just is."

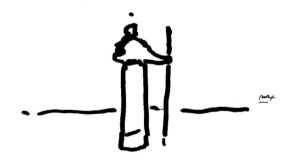

"Spirit is love and it is life. It really is the mystery of life, the glue that holds the universe together. Spirit expresses itself in the way we build relationships with people, how we find our purpose in life, how we fulfill that purpose. Spirit is the ever-present force we are all in tune with. I have always felt that Spirit is guiding me, and I have a sense of being rooted in Spirit."

Gautama (Gotham) Chopra, broadcast journalist, son of Deepak Chopra

"To me, Spirit is the life force that is within us all. It burns brighter for some than others. I think a person can be spiritual without ever setting foot inside a church. It has to do with daring to know yourself, your demons and your angels; and with grasping your significance in the universe, while understanding how insignificant you are ultimately."

Eleanor Clift, contributing editor at *Newsweek*, panelist of *The McLaughlin Group*

"Children are Spirit. If only we could keep that in mind and see, in every child's face, the faith and hopefulness that we see in the image we have of Jesus as the Shepherd. I feel so strongly that we owe our children the chance to have a spiritual life. A recent survey studying young people's drug use found that children who had regular religious involvement and attendance in a church or synagogue were far less likely to engage in self-destructive behavior such as drug use.

"From an awareness that we know only in part, the Spirit of God prods us to look for ways we can work together to help our children.

"All of us who are members of churches and synagogues and mosques should set an example of love and respect. In whatever form it appears in our holy writings, we should follow what I know as 'the Golden Rule.' We would ask all people to act, when outside church, the same way we act inside, and to throw open the church doors after school and on weekends, especially in some of our tougher neighborhoods, so that children have places that are safe to go."

Hillary Clinton, First Lady of the United States

"Spirit connects the life force to the heaven force, creating balance between here and there. Earth and sky are bound together through Spirit. Spirit is true eagle soaring on the wind floating up, up, up to touch the sky. Spirit is the four directions of life."

Chip Comins, producer, director, and president of American Spirit Productions

GERAldINE FERRARO

She lives in our hearts and minds as the first and only woman ever to be nominated to the second-highest office in the land; her legacy as the 1984 Democratic Party nominee for vice president of the United States will live on in our history books. And although her political life was marked by painful blows, no media bashing or attacks in the political arena can keep Geraldine Ferraro down. Recently, she felt guided to jump back into the ring and run again for U.S. senator. Once again, she experienced political defeat. But Ferraro is not defeated. Spirit got her this far, and she has faith that God is the campaign manager of her life!

"My mother used to tell me that if something doesn't work out, I should learn from it and then move on," she says. "That's what life is— moving on. If you focus on the bad experiences and forget there is something ahead, you stop looking for it. If you stop looking for something in the future, then you really stop existing in a productive way. So we have to keep learning, even from the bad experiences."

Ferraro admits she is still a seeker, searching at every turn for spiritual guidance about what to take on next. "I come at this from a very religious background because I was raised that way. I find as I get older that I have no problem still searching for what it is that I'm supposed to be doing to fulfill the reason I'm here. Life is a search ... and I'd better figure it out."

She continues to be a national heroine to many through her activism for women's rights, human rights, and her Democratic Party. She is a highly respected CNN television commentator. Yet it is her devotion to family and religion that truly carried her through many of life's storms. In the hail of controversy that has come her way, the public has rarely glimpsed Ferraro's very private and deep spiritual life.

She says it is her faith that has kept her connected to Spirit since childhood. Recollections of the earliest days of her spiritual awakening sometimes fill her with a sense of longing for the time when things were simpler, when peace was ever-present. She wistfully recalls connecting with a higher power regularly in childhood.

"I was raised in a religious family—in Catholic school and a semi-cloistered convent. I was boarded in, so I grew up believing and expecting and searching. In high school, we used to have weekend retreats where you would go for four days without talking and you spent a lot of time praying and meditating. We were 12, 13, and 14 years old. But I remember how I always felt at peace with everything around me. It was the experience of absolute peace.

"Frequently, I will go to church, sit there, and yearn for the ability to do that again. Now, I do not have the four days. I do not know if that luxury is available anymore—if it were, I would take advantage of it. I don't think you could ever understand that real peace unless you have experienced it, as I did growing up."

Ferraro has heard criticism for many of her career choices and yet appears to feel guided, even though not everything turned out as she would have hoped. "I do think that God speaks to you. I am sure that when I have done some of the things I've done, God has spoken to me and said *this is what you do, this is how you do it.* I have been very fortunate. I have had this hand on my shoulder ever since I was a kid. Obviously, I have lost in some instances. But I do think that there is a reason for everything."

When Ferraro speaks in her no-nonsense style, with that Queens, New York, lilt to her voice, you won't hear her utter phrases such as "guided by" or "embraced by Spirit." Yet she seems to know the essence of Spirit intimately.

What is Spirit? "I rely on my religious background, and I really do believe that God gets me through everything," she says. "To me, *Spirit* certainly has a religious connotation. I do not believe that there are *forces at work* or that there is *energy out there.* I do not believe in that stuff. I do believe that—obviously—there is a God, and I believe that it is a living God who is concerned about my future and the future of every human being. I am not quite sure if I have to give it a gender, but I truly believe there is a God, and I believe that God creates us in His image and puts us here for a reason.

"If God for one second ceased to believe in my existence, I would stop existing. So I think the dependence we have on God is significant, but by the same token, I do not think that God preordains what we do. God gives us options and God puts people in places so they can be helpful. For instance, why was I given a mother like the one I had— this wonderful, guiding woman? I was able to do the things that I could because of her, so, as I said, I think we are all here for a reason."

"I've felt the presence of Spirit when I was visiting children, particularly children with some sort of terminal illness, who are such wonderfully hopeful people. They know that their time is limited in this place, yet that does not diminish the quality of their lives whatsoever. They are grateful for each breath of air they have, and they are such wonderful presences.

"These children seem to open my eyes to the possibilities of what is out there, for myself and everyone. The Spirit I feel from them is the Spirit of positive energy, of continuing on to enjoy every moment. So Spirit is hopefulness in the face of adversity."

Jim Courier, world-class tennis player

"Spirit is that little voice inside you that says, 'Go ahead. You can do it.' And once you do it, it says, 'Have fun!'"

Elliott Curson, president and owner of an advertising agency

"My grandmother, who lived into her 90s, used to say that life is great—if you just don't weaken. What she did not say—only implied—is that Spirit is what keeps you from weakening."

Christine Davies, journalist, author, communications executive

To feel the kiss of the sun, the wind's caress,
to breathe deeply of the scent of the Earth,
To sit near the stars when my work is done,
to hold a baby right after birth,
To be busy all day, making strawberry pie, or
planting a young mango tree,
To be in love always, no matter who I'm with—
that's Spirit flowing in me.

Marilyn Diamond, co-author of the bestseller *Fit for Life* and other books

"Spirit is what enables a person to consciously perceive its interrelationship with all other souls, and the interrelationship of this universal soul/consciousness with the whole of the universe. Spirit is at once an enlightening and a humbling experience, giving one greater appreciation for life and for the role our soul plays in relation to others. Spiritual people are never alone, as they understand their connection with both matter and living things."

Robert Doornick, creator of the business science known as Techno-Marketing™

"Spirit is a gift from God that connects us with God. It comforts us, makes known God's desires for our lives, and gives us a means of communicating with God. It gives joy and peace in times of distress in our lives as well as in good times."

Cindy L. Dorscher, electrician at a chemical company

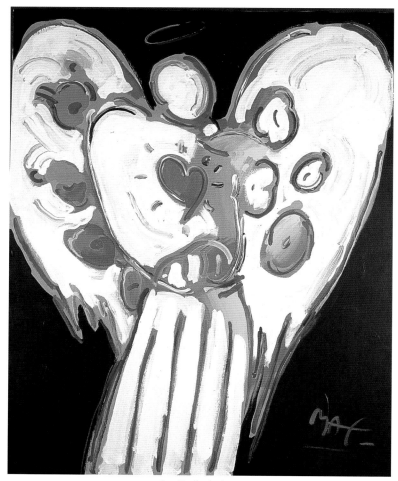

Peter Max "Angel with Heart, Version V, #1" 1995, 60″ x 48″, acrylic on canvas

"Spirit is what connects us to God
and to each other"

Roma Downey

ANNE FREY

Anne Frey is one of those people who inspires others just by her very being. A former flight attendant who flew for 20 years, she admits that much of her life was devoted to self-destructive behavior, crazy relationships with men, unresolved issues with her parents, and escaping pain through drugs and alcohol. Today she is an active and very public member of Alcoholics Anonymous (AA) who regularly lectures to share her experience of strength and hope with other alcoholics and addicts, and with anyone who can benefit. Frey has been clean and sober for about seven years. She lives one day at a time, completely in touch with "a power greater than myself."

"My mother is an active alcoholic. She was suicidal," Frey says. "It was chaos at home. I really felt all alone and very much a victim of my parent's dysfunction." She turned to alcohol and drugs, believing herself unworthy of any kind of spiritual experience. "When I realized that no matter what I did or who I was, I was loved by a power greater than myself, then I had the ability to change."

Before the transformation came the meltdown, when her drug addiction and alcoholism consumed her. Spirit somehow lifted her from the sea of despair so she could get the help she needed.

"I was so lonely, so empty, and so devoid of anything that I really didn't think there was any reason to go on. Then I had what I call a *divine intervention*." She says that "there was a power that came and helped me. You can call it a higher power, Spirit, God. I believe God intervened in my life and decided it wasn't time for me to check out. I ended up in rehab the next day. There I was introduced to AA and to God; it was my reintroduction to a power greater than myself."

After she'd been sober for a year and a half, she was diagnosed with esophageal cancer. "It was June 12, 1994 that I was officially diagnosed. Then, this surgeon told my husband that I had possibly six months to live, to take me home, that I was going to have a very quick and painful death. My husband never told me, which was a very wonderful thing. I mean… I'm here.

"And I am here for a reason: to help other people—addicts, alcoholics, cancer people, other people in life. I have a marvelous, wonderful, happy life. I am so spiritually full of happiness and love. And I truly believe this is because of letting a power greater than myself come into my heart and into my soul. So I try to pass on what has been given to me."

What is Spirit? "I do not have any profound definition of what Spirit or God is. I just know that it is a presence and a being that is true love and kindness. It really is pretty simple for me. I try to smile at everyone I see. I try to speak to people I see. I try to be nonjudgmental. Inside, everyone is like a child of God. We are all here for a reason."

Medically, she says, she is not out of the woods. "I feel great . . . but it has never gone away." She says that the cancer has metastasized and she has several slow-growing tumors in her lungs, and has opted not to have treatment. She was blessed with an oncologist who would not accept her into a trial because he thought the medication would make her sick and steal her spirit and strength.

To her doctors at Sloan-Kettering in New York, she is a medical miracle. "I'm their wonder patient. They come in and just look at me. They do not understand medically why I am still alive. They do not have a clue. They lecture and write about me."

The physicality of cancer is part of daily life. Because she has no esophagus, and due to surgery, digesting food is difficult. "I think about it every day; I cannot say that I do not," she says. "Everything has changed—and it is wonderful. My priorities have all shifted. What I really need are my family and my friends and honesty and compassion and peace. I found such a peace that I never, ever had before.

"Spirit presents itself at different times now, in different ways." Frey says. "I look at my diseases—alcoholism, drug addiction, and cancer—as a gift. I am so grateful to have cancer. Not that I welcome it into my body and say, 'You can stay,' but it has changed me spiritually. I do not think that this possibly could have happened to me otherwise. So I do not have any anger. I've let anger go.

"I was so afraid of dying, and that has been lifted from me. I do not have a fear of death. I have a fear of missing the people I love—my family, my daughter, and my husband. And I fear for the pain and heartache that my leaving will put them through. That is what is upsetting to me, but I am really excited about what is next."

"Spirit is what allows certain people to maintain that higher ground while overcoming *most* of the temptations that life puts in our way."

William J. Doyle, chairman of a construction company

"Let me give you a metaphor: Close your eyes and imagine the most magnificent fireworks, and then make them get bigger and broader than your imagination can deal with. One glowing spark zooms down to Earth and brings life to a leaf on a tree—the leaf suddenly understands what it is and what simply being is. Another spark flies down and enters a woman's womb, and life begins, and for that spark the learning may be forgiveness—for you cannot get to beingness until you get through forgiveness. That spark is Spirit. It is that force within us, before us, after us, the forever everywhere force that miraculously, invisibly, is just there. That continues in a continuum where the miracle of life is simply one of its journeys—and is Spirit."

Dr. Barry Dubin, has a doctorate in dentistry and a master's in psychology

"Spirit is the still, small voice in all of us that reminds us, over and over, that we are loved by God."

John Dye, TV actor who plays the kind-hearted Angel of Death
on *Touched by an Angel*

"I talk to kids about living and dying. Many have a lack of appreciation for life; they feel it really doesn't matter how long you live as long as you have a good time while you're here. You tell them, 'If you stay in these groups and with the drug stuff, you're gonna die.' They say, 'You gotta die sometime.' We give them an opportunity to find some kind of a value system, and a vision that has a future. I would like to inspire them toward the possibility of living a full life. To be creative and find joy in ways that are not destructive, and to participate in some kind of an exchange of love, caring, and respect.

"To watch a mean, angry, don't-touch-me look turn into a warm, loving smile—now that's Spirit."

Father John Flynn, parish priest who helped found
a nondenominational program for kids

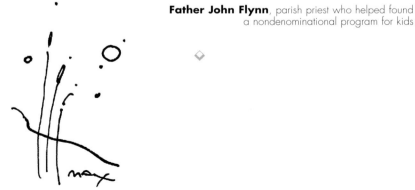

"Every human being has a spirit within them. It's something that makes us be what we are... My husband and I never would have made the change in our lives that led to establishing Habitat for Humanity without the encouragement and the calling of the Holy Spirit. That Spirit guided us along the way as this ministry developed. It feeds us, nourishes us, and gives us strength when we get discouraged. Spirit is there all the time."

Linda Fuller (See below)

"There's incredible Spirit in the work we do. There's a commonality of purpose, a specific assignment: to build houses for families in need. Here you've got Spirit translated into action. It's what Jesus did. Jesus was the ultimate in spirituality. He taught that if somebody's thirsty, you don't go have a prayer service for her; you give her water. If somebody's hungry, feed him. Those expressions of love in real situations represent the ultimate in Spirit. That's what happens at a Habitat work site. You're out there interacting with the homeowners, eating lunch with them, saying prayers, driving nails, and laying blocks with them. At the end of the week, everybody's hugging each other, crying, shouting, and laughing, and there's a sense of community. It's filled with Spirit."

Milliard Fuller, Linda and Milliard Fuller are co-founders of Habitat for Humanity

Gloria Gaynor

Gloria Gaynor rose to stardom in the '70s with "I Will Survive," the song that immortalized her and heralded a new era for disco internationally. She was crowned "Disco Queen" and rode high on the disco wave until life brought her down another path; what first looked like failure turned out to be a gift from Spirit, in disguise.

Heartache set in not long after her star began to rise. Her mother—a great support and anchor—passed away; her death set the stage for Gloria's struggle with weight, drugs, and alcohol. She suffered financial devastation; she also suffered from low self-esteem. Then in the early '80s, supported by her husband, Linwood Simon, and guided by her mother's old Bible, she began a spiritual quest that would take her on visits to many churches, where she discovered the world of gospel music—and salvation.

"I think the strongest feeling that I ever had about Spirit was God prompting me to read the Bible—just moments before I became a born-again Christian," she says. "That force was so strong that I just could not resist it. Then God began to lead me: *Okay, open to this. Now open to that.* To me, that was absolutely, undeniably God, because I didn't know where anything was in the Bible."

What is Spirit? "It is the essence of being, an essence of God. I find that it's closely connected with Christ only because I believe he is the author of the human spirit. He is the creator of the human spirit. He breathes into the form that he made, and it becomes a living spirit."

In finding God, Gaynor found meaning for her successes and losses of the past; they were building blocks for spiritual leadership. "I believe that 'I Will Survive' was a gift from God," she says. "A gift that he planned to use later. I feel that he will use it even more because it has made me well known and popular in more than 80 countries. It has made me a symbol of strength and courage, and even of truth, integrity, and self-esteem to a lot of people. So when I'm ready to go into full ministry, I think a lot more people will be able to accept hearing about the Lord from me because of what they know of me already."

A few years ago she re-recorded her classic song to include a new first line: *Only the Lord could give me strength not to fall apart*. Her comeback, performing and traveling on tour with her book, *I Will Survive*, has also been a rebirth—from Disco Queen to minister. She plans to become an ordained minister—to serve "the sexually and relationally broken." She adds, "I'm going to minister to couples and individuals and children and whoever God brings my way."

She envisions the creation of a Christian-based family center that would "draw everybody." It's aimed at Christians and inner-city children, and will be a place to have fun and learn life skills, as well as "form and perform in relationships."

Gloria says that "this place I am thinking of is huge. I am thinking about a sports bar for men that serves nonalcoholic drinks. And a video-game room for teenagers, and a romper room for babies and toddlers. There will be marriage, premarital, and ethics classes. You can be there from nine in the morning until four in the morning. And you can bring the entire family. You don't even have to pay to come to this place. I see it as not-for-profit. A nightclub on the premises, where Christian acts and clean secular acts perform, will help raise money.

"It is hard, when you're an entertainer, to know if a vision is rising up from your ego or coming from the Lord," she says. "But I am not trying to pull it off. I know the Lord can pull it off."

"The essence and consciousness of one's soul—dark and enlightened. Both extremes are vital and should be left to flourish unrestricted. For in that journey discoveries are made."

Andy Garcia, film actor

"Spirit is a part of God … God wants us to be happy. And God made us all. And everyone's not born with one leg like me; I have a prosthetic leg. Everyone's not born the same way because God wants us to be different all the time. So I think Spirit is a joyful thing. We should pray for it. And God is wonderful. I think we go to church and pray for Him so He feels better. He likes when we pray for Him. It's a joyful occasion. Or it could be a she. But we should pray for whatever God. And that's what Spirit is."

Alexander Kent Garrett, age 7

"The life force; that part of our being that transcends the physiology of the neurochemical reactions and defines brain and nervous system function; the substance of love, passion, and caring."

Neil Goodman, M.D., physician who specializes in reproductive medicine

"Spirit is that loving, creative intelligence at the core of all life, always sustaining us. It is the True Self, that source which we have never left, only forgotten."

Henry Grayson, Ph.D., chairman of The Center for Spirituality and Psychotherapy

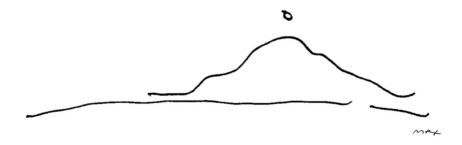

Peter Max "Angel with Heart Version I, #1" 1993, 36″ x 24″, acrylic on canvas

"There is an essence of the divine in all living things.
And each person is literally
a microcosm of the universe"

Gloria Steinem

JEREMY GEFFEN

Spiritual hunger gripped Jeremy Geffen at age 16 and set him on a search for answers to the deepest questions about the meaning of life and death.

His spiritual quest led him to explore Judaism with an orthodox rabbi, Buddhism with a Zen Master, and yoga and meditation with a Hindu spiritual teacher. His spiritual longing was so great that at age 19 he went to live for four years in an ashram (spiritual community) and embraced the Eastern traditions of Hinduism and Tibetan Buddhism. After diving deeply into the realms of Eastern spirituality, his life took another course. He moved to Manhattan and got an undergraduate degree at Columbia University, before enrolling in New York University School of Medicine and becoming a physician.

In love with science and medicine and yet firmly grounded in his spirituality, Geffen refused to choose one over the other. He knew that his path was to become a bridge between skillful medicine and wise spiritual traditions. "Early on in medical school, it became clear to me that my path in medicine would be based in oncology, because cancer patients and their families are right on the edge of the two worlds. They need meticulous, impeccable medical care—but, quite often, they're also literally staring into the abyss of the unknown, so they need love, wisdom, and incredible kindness as well."

Ironically, when Geffen was in his last year of medical school, his father was diagnosed with cancer and died less than four months later. "I got to live the problem and the challenge that people with cancer go through from the point of view of a family member, and it was unimaginably painful," he recalls. "During the process of walking that road with him, the vision of what I was going to do with my career became crystal clear. There was no cancer center where patients could go and get the best of both worlds, so I decided to create one myself."

Geffen went on to complete residency training in internal medicine at the University of California at San Diego Medical Center, followed by fellowship training in hematology and oncology at the University of California at San Francisco Medical Center, and became a board-certified medical oncologist. Throughout his training he also traveled to India, Nepal, China, and Tibet, and continued his studies of the spiritual and healing traditions of the East. He finally opened the doors of the Geffen Cancer Center and Research Institute in Vero Beach, Florida, in 1994.

His goal was to create an environment that could offer the best of conventional as well as alternative, complementary, and mind/body therapies, while at the same time embracing the central role of love, Spirit, and consciousness in the healing process. The Center's fundamental principle is this: Human beings have a body, but they also have a mind, a heart, and a spirit. And if healing and transformation is to occur at the deepest levels, *every* dimension of who they are has to be addressed with equal skill and integrity.

Geffen's approach to caring for cancer patients is grounded in state-of-the-art conventional medicine. But, along with a variety of alternative, complementary, and mind/body therapies, it also includes encouraging people to explore and connect with what is most important to them in their lives. "For many people, receiving a diagnosis of cancer is like smashing into a brick wall after years and years of effort, activity, and searching for happiness in the external world, always wondering why they are never quite happy," he says. "Thus, one of our main goals is to give them the very best possible medical care, while at the same time helping them discover how to find the love and joy they seek *within themselves,* regardless of their circumstances. Part of that process involves looking inside and asking: What is the meaning and purpose of my life? What is truly important to me? What do I really care about the most? Do I want to live? If so, why?"

Many people initially have some difficulty answering these questions because they haven't thought about them in a clear, conscious way," he says. "But with love, support, and proper guidance they can definitely find the answers they need to move forward. The process of exploring a person's true desire and commitment to live or not to live is delicate and deep. Most often this exploration leads individuals to much more meaningful and healthier lives—and it is beautiful to facilitate and see this process unfold. Occasionally, some individuals will come to the heartfelt conclusion that they are truly ready to let go of life as we know it, and we can then help them focus on completing their journey in the most loving, harmonious, and elegant way.

"The greatest discovery of all," Geffen says, "is when patients and loved ones begin to discover a deeper truth about *who they really are* at the deepest level—beyond the level of appearances. We are not our bodies, our thoughts, or our emotions—even though it often feels like we are, especially when we are ill. We take ourselves to be separate beings, like individual waves on the ocean—when in fact we are the ocean itself. When you know yourself as the ocean, rather than the wave, you can handle and respond to whatever life brings you—no matter how challenging—with less pain and fear, and with much greater love, confidence, and inner peace. Helping individuals discover that freedom within themselves brings *me* great joy, and makes it all worthwhile."

"Spirit is not something that you can see, smell, or taste. Most of the time when we feel it, it scares us because we do not know what it is. It is part of our human consciousness. It is the Force of God—what created the whole universe. It has nothing to do with religion. When you understand it, then you tap into it. It is Spirit that goes in and heals folks when they are sick. In the civil rights movement, I thought good Spirit was when one was right and somebody else was wrong. But when I saw Nelson Mandela walk out of jail with no hatred and no bitterness, I realized he had authentic Spirit. That touched me. I believe that when you are quiet, Spirit will come and run rampant through your body. Spirit knows all. All I have to do is be still, quiet and listen, and Spirit will come to me and heal what needs to be healed; it will throw out what needs to be thrown out. It will wipe away all the fears and anxiety."

Dick Gregory, civil and human rights activist, comedian

"Spirit is the essence of the light force of God, which is in each and every one of us. In fact, it is the part of us that orchestrates our entire personal universe, to bring to ourselves that which we need to heal our soul and find our way back to God. This seed of God, which resides within us, leads to our destiny. Spirit is the light that guides our interior journey through the veil of ignorance across the bridge to Enlightenment."

Gail Gross, humanitarian, savvy businesswoman, scholar

"Spirit to me is the indefinable thing that makes human life so wonderful. It's the sense of love, of anticipation; it's the beauty of life. It's the thing that gives you an extra-special joy, like the singular joy you get when you see your children succeeding and doing well. Spirit is getting up in the morning and seeing that it's a beautiful day, and thanking God that you're alive and that you have the ability to participate. I think Spirit is also a sense of hope and optimism that, no matter how bad things are, they may get better. I think that's very much a part of the human Spirit. I think that's what human beings contribute to the world."

Rudolph Giuliani, mayor of New York City

"Spirit is a feeling, a sixth sense, another person inside, cheering, talking you on through. It is a smile, a twinkle; you know it and like it!"

Steve Guttenberg, actor who has played many spirited roles

"Spirit, to me, is the awakening of one's own inner connection to the divine-seeing God in the all-being one with the all-earth-universe … Spirit gives us the courage, power, strength, and wisdom to be here to perform our work."

Joanne W. Haahr, president of a networking company

"Spirit is all in which our bodies house … It's an inner strength that gives us the courage to do what we must, and a self-love that gives us the belief that we can. It's the driving force behind all that we do and all that we are."

Patricia Hankin, real estate sales associate, domestic engineer

JOSEPH GELBERMAN

Rabbi Joseph Gelberman is a passionate pioneer and teacher of the interfaith approach to Spirit and worship. Raised in the Hasidic tradition and also a master of mystical Judaism, the Kabbalah, he was led by Spirit to create a forum for interfaith teachings in the '70s called the New Seminary in New York. Upon his recent retirement at age 87, he founded the All Faiths School for Children, a program designed for interfaith couples who want to teach their children how to appreciate their heritage and to worship God through more than one religion.

The rabbi has been on a unique mission to unite people of all faiths and to do his part to end hatred, killing, destruction, and all forms of religious persecution. A spiritual leader known for his wisdom and humor, he comes to his mission through his own profound experiences with religious persecution—as a child in Hungary, and then again as a young rabbi, when his wife and young daughter were taken to Auschwitz by Nazis, never to be seen again.

Discovering Spirit was never an issue. Spirit was with him from the very start. "I come from a Hasidic background, and you live God every moment of your life," he says. "God is real and necessary because it is almost what you would call a hateful environment. Anti-Semitism surrounds you. As a child we'd walk miles to a Hebrew school, and my family never knew if I would come home alive; many times I would come home with blood all over my face because I would pass a church and they would throw stones. So in that environment, God is very real because the only hope we had was that God would somehow interfere and keep us safe. We know God is there because I'm still alive."

Rabbi Gelberman embraces the idea that although religions are different, the intention is always the same—getting close to God. He likes to illustrate his interfaith philosophy in the following way for the many students he has trained: "Imagine a blackboard, and in the middle of the blackboard are the names of all the religions. Over the list of religions is a big 'G,' meaning 'God.' When you look at it, you realize we're all going to the same place. Let's help each other to get there."

What is Spirit? Spirit is choice, and embracing joy. "The Buddha said that suffering is a part of life. So we also suffer, but I don't pay attention to that. I rejoice because it is a sign that I am still alive. If I did not feel anything, I would be dead. It came to me after the Holocaust—where I lost my family, my wife, my child, everything. I had a choice. Everybody has this choice. Either you continue to mourn for the rest of your life, and you see only the dark side of life, or you say, 'I cannot do anything about them anymore, but I can enrich my own life.' In my case I continue their life in my life. Therefore, I add as much joy as I can, and I recognize that joy is the thing that God wants me to live."

Rabbi Gelberman has been a chaplain in the United States Army and had many traditional pulpits. His last was in Princeton, where he got a visit from Spirit. "I was there for three years, and I was always a good pastor. And one day, I don't know how it happened, but I heard my soul crying. And the cry was, 'You're fine, you're doing well, but you're really not doing anything for yourself. You're serving the congregation, but you're really not growing.' The message was to leave the traditional pulpit and go on my own."

He came back to New York and took an apartment, where he taught classes. Then came several small congregations, and eventually the Little Synagogue, a memorial synagogue that operated on the High Holy days and other times when the dead were remembered. Today, he runs his own small and cozy congregation, the New Synagogue. It is not rare to find many people of other faiths greeting the Sabbath with the rabbi. All are welcome, and worship is free to all.

"It was through my mother's death that I learned what Spirit is and found peace at last. She was not at all afraid at the end, and neither was I. I held her hand as she slipped away and knew that she was only leaving Earth. She would never leave me. Her spirit is as familiar to me now, and as present, as it was when she died. I have never missed her comfort. I have only missed being unable to make new memories on Earth with her."

Dianne Harper, dental practice manager

"The most important property of Spirit is belief. I say this because I believe that a strong will can bring about a strong outcome—when you believe, your Spirit taps into cosmic energy (Allah) and that belief is given form, substance, and ultimately life. They say 'where there's a will, there's a way'— but that is because there's belief."

Alimayu Harris, senior account executive with Wall Street Strategies

"Spirit is my heart. I learned that when my father died in 1988. He was everything to me. He was my strength, my wisdom, who I wanted to be. When he died, my security died. So I had to take the journey and go live in the mountains by myself for one year. I lived up in the mountains with a pack of wolves, and the wolves taught me who I was. After I did the vision quest, I realized I was secure; my father was in me. From that point on, I walked with Spirit. I take the hand of Spirit and I am Spirit. And the Spirit has declared that my conviction is peace, and I will see that the children on this planet have peace, forever."

Cynthia Hart, half-Lakota medicine woman from Sedona, Arizona

"From the most simple pleasures—like the smile on a dog, the joy in a child's eyes, or a delicate flower blowing in the gentle wind—to the most grand, like a majestic mountain range, powerful mother ocean, or a sunset fading into a star-filled sky, Spirit reminds me that it is everywhere, always."

Kim Hart, artist, producer

"My intuition tells me that Spirit is to be found in that place where biology and physics converge. That Spirit is a highly rarefied form of matter—energy that is actually capable of conducting Consciousness—Awareness—Life. The Universe, and everything in it, is probably saturated with this most mysterious and most common substance. It is the Divine in the highest and the lowest, the great and the small. It is our birthright and our One True Calling."

Damon Eric Harvey, small business owner

"Spirit is getting up in the morning with a feeling of joy and excitement about the new day, rather than feeling depressed or anxious. Spirit is feeling a sense of confidence and inner peace, rather than worrying about what other people think of you. Spirit is living life in the moment with a feeling of gratitude and connectedness to the world, rather than living mostly in mental movies about the past and the future. But mostly, Spirit is opening the heart and seeing the best in myself and in other people, rather than being clogged with judgments. The best measure of a full life is not in its length, but in its love."

David A. Hawley, professor of geography

Robin and Dwina Gibb

Robin and Dwina Gibb share a spiritual path in their marriage. Each one experienced Spirit very early in age. Robin accessed Spirit through writing music as a child and creating, with his brothers Maurice and Barry, what would become the Bee Gees. Dwina found Spirit through prayer and trying to visualize a clear picture of the divine.

"Music is my religion," Robin says. "It is very spiritual. I get from hearing a piece of music what most people probably get from religion. To me it is a very powerful spiritual motivator."

Music, he says, has Spirit all its own. "I have spoken to Paul McCartney and other writers, and they have experienced the same feeling. It's like you're taking notation from another source. It's something that gets stronger. You just do it."

The death of his younger brother Andy crystallized his sense of Spirit. "It made me more aware of my spirituality. I knew the body's life was very short, and that Spirit was forever. It made me feel that time on Earth, in bodies, should be valued and used to nourish the spirit."

What is Spirit? "Spirit is that thing you feel beyond anything physical. That is why I think music affects the spirit more than the physical body, because it is an organized kind of sound, a vibration. Vibrations on a certain type of rhythm will actually affect the soul. And there is a sense of forever about it, a sense of going on and on, a sense of eternity."

Peter Max "Hearts #1" 1992, 16″ x 16″, acrylic on canvas

"I get from hearing a piece of music
what most people probably get from religion.
To me it is a very spiritual motivator"

Robin Gibb

Dwina says she has always felt that Spirit was guiding her. "When I was very young, I desperately wanted to see God. I didn't quite believe this image of a big fellow with this big black book writing down good and bad deeds. I had a vision when I was about eight years old that changed my mind to thinking in terms of God being the cycles of life. The concept of God as a judge slipped away because I wanted to feel love. Even though I loved life when I was young, and I still do, I always felt disassociated, like this wasn't my real home."

Over time, Spirit guided her to a teacher who brought her home to God, and she entered a spiritual practice of meditation and yoga with great commitment. In 1998, she further committed to the path by becoming a Brahman, through the Brahma Kumaris Spiritual University.

For Dwina, it is the yogic practice of life as a Brahman that brings her the experience of being one with all that is. "Many yogas teach about enlightenment and reaching the light," she says. "In this practice you actually see the light, and can be in that light, listen to it, hear it, and find knowledge—fast. You don't have to sit in a cave for ten years. In a moment of silence, it is as if I plug into a battery—and everything flows."

What is Spirit? "Total, unlimited love and happiness," says Dwina.

"Since I was a very young girl, the Holy Spirit has been a real guiding light for my life. For me, it's so easy to understand, but it can be difficult to explain it to someone else. In my experience, when you are filled with Spirit it is contagious. It's like an eternal flame that people are drawn to. It's the smile from you that someone needs and didn't expect, generous giving without expecting something in return, when you're singing a song or communicating with an audience, the ability to get out of the way and let the Spirit move through you to someone else. To me, Spirit is that light that shines so bright in people's eyes. One of the greatest things about Spirit is that it doesn't notice the color of a person's skin, what religion they belong to, their age, or their financial status. I couldn't imagine life without the Holy Spirit, for Spirit is life and life is Spirit."

Florence Henderson, singer, actress, and everyone's favorite mom on *The Brady Bunch*

"We nurture our soul by giving and receiving love, and by learning to be present in each moment. The Spirit then comes alive within us and touches those around us. When we open to the Spirit and attend to our soul, we feel in touch with wonder, delight, and inspiration, and we live our lives with authenticity and gratitude."

Sharon Hills-Bonczyk, director of family resources at a children's hospital

"The Spirit, or *a* Spirit, is that entity which *is* the individual, separate and distinct from the individual's mind and body. The Spirit, or individual, has greater or lesser degrees of awareness on many levels and has infinite abilities that, depending on the individual's experiences, conclusions, and decisions, may be occluded or 'dampened' to various degrees. Many teach that Man has a soul, whereas I prefer to think that Man *is* a soul. (Not bad for an engineer, eh?)"

Mark Hinspeter, automobile engineer

"I believe Spirit to be an energy or force in the universe that unites all living things. We, as continually evolving humans, have an opportunity to explore a more conscious type of spirituality. Most of us have at times felt spiritually moved, whether in a church, synagogue, or sanctuary. Maybe sitting alone in the stillness of the desert or nature, or sharing and connecting with others around us. I believe that at those times we can sense the oneness that unites all of life. Spirit, I believe, flows through us and transcends time and space. Spirit . . . pure conscious light."

Tony Hochstetler, small business owner and manager

"Spirit makes you succeed when everything else fails. (I have some jokes in my files that could have used a little Spirit.)"

Bob Hope, world-renowned comedian, entertainer, actor

"Spirit is the art of living fully, in the moment, and realizing the interconnectedness of all people, to each other and the natural world. Spirit is what motivates individuals to create and share deeply, and what gives meaning to daily struggle."

James Horowitz, executive producer

"Spirit is a reflection of a reflection, the echo of eternity that lights our conscience, reveals our purpose, and steels our resolve."

James Humes, author of 24 books; speechwriter for five U.S. presidents

A. LEON HIGGINBOTHAM

The Honorable A. Leon Higginbotham was revered by many. His tireless efforts on behalf of civil rights helped to reshape our nation. He was asked by U.S. presidents and other world leaders to serve justice. President John F. Kennedy appointed him the first black member of the Federal Trade Commission in 1962. President Jimmy Carter elevated him to the Third U.S. Circuit Court of Appeals in 1977, where he served until 1993. In 1994, South African president Nelson Mandela asked him to mediate during the country's first elections in which blacks could vote.

The judge received the highest civilian honor, the Presidential Honor of Freedom, in 1995. One of his final acts before his death, in December 1998, was to testify on behalf of President Bill Clinton and argue that the president's actions did not rise to the level of an impeachable offense.

"My husband was always concerned about the plight of people who have not enjoyed the fruits of all that this nation has to offer," recalls Evelyn Brooks Higginbotham, author and historian, who shared a wonderful 15-year marriage with Justice Higginbotham. "He fought so tirelessly for justice for those in need. He was an advocate for justice. He was a lawyer, a writer. He spoke out. He was not afraid to take a position in the face of unpopularity. He was such a soldier."

In Judge Higginbotham's final moments, President Clinton called from Jerusalem. "I'm just decimated," he told Mrs. Higginbotham. "Leon touched so many lives," she says. "I shared my husband with a lot of people. They all felt the loss."

The judge's death was a peaceful letting-go that led his wife to see Spirit in a new and profound way. He slipped away as his family stood around him. "When they took the life support off, he breathed—not a laborious breathing, just a very kind of simple breathing, that just faded out," she recalls. "It wasn't a traumatic kind of experience for us, watching him, because he was so peaceful.

"I believe my husband's spirit is still alive. I believe my husband's spirit is still with me and that it is still present—that it is immortal. It gives me a sense of hope for my own demise as a human being on this Earth—that the spirit within me will continue," Mrs. Higginbotham says.

What is Spirit? Mrs. Higginbotham answers on his behalf: "For my husband, it was recognizable in his tremendous optimism. No matter what adversities he faced, he always stood up to them. When he was a little boy, he wanted to be a fireman; his uncles said, 'You can't because they don't have any colored people on the fire department.' His mother rebutted, 'If you can't encourage him, don't discourage him.' She had tremendous belief in what he could be. She saw within him this kind of energy, this kind of Spirit. He always used to say that he got his Spirit from his mother."

Mrs. Higginbotham adds, "It was the Spirit in him that didn't let him quit or be daunted or discouraged. My husband believed very much in God; he saw within himself the power given by God to do the things he could. He had a strong faith, an unwavering belief that it's going to work. That's what he did, right up until the end of his life."

◇ ◇

"Spirit is the capacity you have to 'negotiate' the world because of your absolute belief that a supreme being is present at all times.

"Spirit is your awareness of the constant presence of God and trust in God's wisdom."

Christine L. James-Brown, president of The United Way of Philadelphia

"Our true identity is Spirit, not body. Spirit is the essence of our being—love. It is synonymous with soul and is a nonphysical form of an energy force that is a mirror reflection of the eternal, unconditional love that is created by the God Source that is within each of us.

"We believe that the Spirit, the soul in each of us, never dies, and is joined with each other and God as One. This Godly Love makes up our Spirit and continues to expand and unfold upon itself. Remembering and recognizing our Oneness with the Source allows us to experience our truest reality, that of Spiritual Beings having a human experience."

Gerald Jampolsky, M.D.; and **Diane V. Cirincione, Ph.D.,**
internationally known authors, lecturers, and teachers of *A Course in Miracles*

"The body and soul together make up a human being. Perceiving ourselves as the immortal Spirit, or the soul, our relationship with nature starts with our bodies and every action that we perform affects the physical matter that our bodies are made of. It also has some effect on all other matter around us. Thus, the state of the matter around us (and the condition of the world as a whole) is a reflection, not just of the quality of our actions, but also of the state of well-being of the soul.

"At the heart of all conflict between nations, groups, and individuals is the profound peacelessness of the human heart as it grasps for meaning and fulfillment by attachment with external, impermanent things, rather than with the eternal truth concerning God, the soul, and the dreams of life."

B. K. Dadi Janki, one of India's first female spiritual leaders

"Spirit is the divine spark inside each human being that connects us to each other, to the universe, and ultimately, back to God. It is the golden thread that connects us to our very souls."

Michelle Johnson-Houghton, certified health-education specialist

What is Spirit?

Spirit is the intangible essence deep within us,

To which, oftentimes, we must stretch our hearts and souls

Hopefully, to realize our life's purpose.

When, momentarily, finding it,

We are revived, freed, and joyous.

And then, sometimes, we are surprised

To find we have been given so much

Understanding from extending ourselves,

We are able to give it away, gladly, to another seeker.

And we are fulfilled.

We realize we are joined, forever together,

Us Humans.

Kathryn K. Hartney, purser and flight attendant

"I believe that being a child of God is my truest identity. My Spirit is eternal! Spirit is the breath of God, a universal energy that, once created, can never be destroyed."

Wynonna Judd, ever-popular country music star

"Spirit is the sense I have about my dad—long after his body left here. My dad died three years ago—I still feel his indomitable Spirit. Spirit is the awesome power emerging from my sister as she battles breast cancer— I feel her indomitable Spirit. Spirit is also a rush of pure energy and joy, embracing every cell in my body—when all is right with my world—Spirit makes life so compelling."

Elisabeth Hope Kalogris, writer

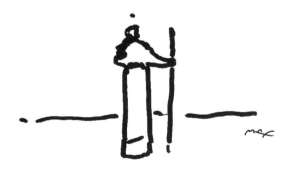

About Richard Hoyt

Richard Hoyt, at age 20, and his now-ex-wife Judy, at 19, were moments away from the eagerly anticipated birth of their first baby, when fate altered the course of their lives—and the lives of people they would eventually touch.

"The umbilical cord got twisted around his neck," says Richard Hoyt, describing the birth of his son, Richard Jr. "He was in such a position that it took minutes for the doctors to get him out and get the cord untangled, causing a lack of oxygen to Rick's brain. At the time, we knew there was something wrong, but we did not know exactly what."

Eight months later, a specialist gave them the painful answer. Rick was diagnosed with cerebral palsy, a condition so serious that the doctors recommended that they institutionalize their baby. "They said he would be nothing but a vegetable for the rest of his life. We had never heard the words *cerebral palsy* before, had never seen anybody in a wheelchair," Hoyt recalls. "On the way home from the doctor's office, we cried, but we said, 'No, we are not going to put Rick away. We are going to bring Rick home and bring him up like any other child.'"

And so they did—fighting for his inclusion in regular school programs, encouraging him to follow his own dreams. Rick's sense of humor, intelligence, and spirit became apparent early. When a lacrosse player at school was in an auto accident and paralyzed from the waist down, Rick wanted to run in a race that had been organized to help raise money for the injured student.

"Dad, I want to do something to help him. Will you run in the race with me?" Hoyt recalls Rick asking him. "I was 40 years old and I was not a runner, except to try to keep weight off. And Rick had his wheelchair, which was form-fitted to his body. But we went down to the race, and they gave us the number double zero. It was a five-mile race. Everybody thought Rick and I would just go down to the corner and turn around and come back."

Instead, they finished the race, and Rick was joyous. "At home that night, Rick wrote on his computer, 'Dad, when I'm running it feels like I am not even handicapped.' Hoyt, on the other hand, couldn't move for two weeks. Clearly, if they were ever to run again, they needed a better racing vehicle.

It took planning and a lot of Spirit to create the Running Chair. From there, father and son went on to run the Boston Marathon. Despite initial skepticism—they were shunted to the back of the wheelchair entries by organizers—and the challenge of it all, they carved out a place for their unusual team: Rick in the Running Chair and Hoyt pushing it forward. They recently completed their 19th Boston Marathon, as well as yet another Iron Man Triathlon in Kona, Hawaii.

"I think there's a Spirit that's been with us for just about all of Rick's life, through the ups and downs," says Hoyt, a retired Air Force lieutenant colonel. "It is just amazing the things we've been able to accomplish. Somebody is up there helping us."

Rick is now 37 and living a very hectic life. A graduate of Boston University, he works at the college computer lab designing computers. A new product, called Legal Eyes, which is controlled with eyes or head movement, holds a patent inspired by Rick's ideas. He teaches youngsters with disabilities how to use the computer and also works at Children's Hospital in Boston, helping them design and work on computers for people with disabilities. He honors many speaking engagements—with his dad or on his own—and he doesn't even speak! He uses a computer with a head switch and a voice synthesizer that speaks for him when he types in words. He's been living on his own since graduating from college.

What is Spirit? "To me, Spirit is my son," Hoyt says. "He's just an unbelievable guy. He's got this thing inside him, and he just gives me the spirit to go and achieve things that people never thought we would be able to do. All of Rick's life everybody said, 'No, you can't do this, you can't do that.' I think he does have a mission because we're traveling all over the world now competing and doing a lot of speaking engagements. He is just out there, and he wants people with disabilities to be treated like everybody else."

Rick typed this answer about Spirit: "It has different meanings for me personally. One is that God watches over all of us. Another is class spirit, where a whole school gets behind their sports teams. A third is the Spirit I experienced once in my life, in June 1983, the year I graduated from high school and received my diploma—my whole class gave me a standing ovation. Fourth is the human spirit, which I feel I have. When nothing is going your way, you have to dig deep within yourself and give something extra. To sum up, I would have to say Spirit is a combination of strong belief in God and the ability to dig deep within yourself to find that something extra."

◇ ◇

"Spirit is like the atom in the physical world. As an atom represents the essence of life in the physical world, Spirit is the essence of life in another realm. In order to see an atom, we must look through a powerful microscope. In order to see Spirit, we must look into ourselves, and then we will see Spirit through our faith and inner beliefs. Spirit is the unique link embodied in all of us, that which God created in His own image and we share through love, trust, and faith in God."

Tom Kann, president of a telecommunications firm

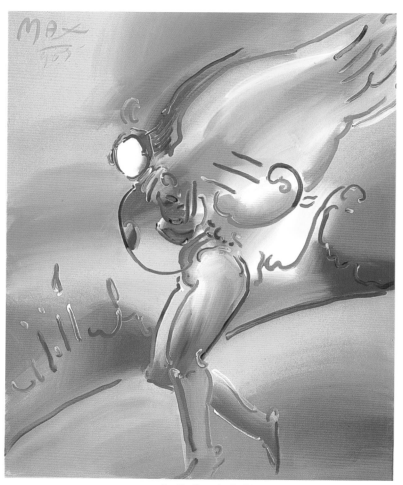

Peter Max "Descending Angel, Version I, #1" 1989, 60″ x 48″, acrylic on canvas

"Spirit is a reflection of a reflection,
the echo of eternity that lights our conscience,
reveals our purpose and steels our resolve"

James Humes

"Spirit is the authenticity of a human being—the inner self revealed with no masks to hide behind. Spirit is passion, goodness, and hopefully someone's soul. This, of course, can only be understood by another who also possesses this extraordinary quality, and it should be shared."

Arlan Mintz Kardon, matrimonial attorney

"Spirit is the realization that the body has a soul within which all the good that God expects is stored. It is the conscious awareness of that soul that can and should dictate our actions and love for our fellow humankind."

Lewis Katz, managing partner of the New Jersey Nets

"Spirit is that agent of transformation which unendingly brings us to the awareness of our possibilities to attain authentic power—to free us from the prison of our illusions (belief systems born of the mind) and the mind's power to control our creativity."

William T. Kelly, D.C., chiropractic physician

DOMINIQUE LAPIERRE

It has been 18 years since Spirit moved journalist and author Dominique Lapierre to reach out to help the people of India. Since then he has contributed to help 9,000 leper children. He has dug 541 wells of drinking water. He has helped to eradicate tuberculosis in 1,200 villages of Bengal. As he explains, "It's a case where a witness, a man who writes about the situations of the world, becomes an actor to change the bad ones."

The journey that transformed him from detached reporter to dedicated humanitarian began the day he felt compelled to seek out Mother Teresa and ask how he could best help the children with leprosy in her country. She guided him toward a man who was doing just that in a profound and touching way. Lapierre would identify this man as a hero, and in fact soon become one himself, trading his days of roaming the planet in search of great human epics for a new life: rolling up his sleeves and making an impact on the human lives he once only wrote about.

"In 1981, with my wife, I went to Calcutta with a share of my royalties to give it to an institution caring for leper children," he says. "This was the beginning of an involvement, a crusade, which for the last 18 years has grown. I was to write a book called *City of Joy* after my encounter with the real heroes of this world and a slum called by that same name in Calcutta."

With Larry Collins, he co-authored *Is Paris Burning?* as well as *Oh, Jerusalem, Freedom from Midnight,* and *The Fifth Horseman*; on his own, he produced the movie *City of Joy,* starring Patrick Swayze. It is a tale of a doctor whose life is transformed by the people of India; it reflects Lapierre's own transformation from detached observer to active participant.

He feels moved by something far greater than himself to do these good works. "I certainly realize I could take part in changing some of the injustices and the hate of this world," he says. "It was not enough only to report about it, to write about the terrible situations in this world; I could also do something to change the situation."

What is Spirit? "Spirit to me is the capacity to bring compassion, a fraternal hand, to those people whose lives you can be instrumental in changing."

Of his work, Lapierre says, "It's a drop of water in the ocean of need." Mother Teresa once assured him that every drop is important. On the day he took his first major step toward the crusade that would become a life's mission, she said to him, "The ocean is made of drops of water."

◇ ◇

"Spirit is God's love within each and every one of us. We are born with it, and it continues after death into a new life. We can count on it to see us through the happy times, as well as the depths of our own anger turned inward. Spirit is the flame within that never goes out. It is God's passion to live love, even as we die. Spirit connects each of our unique beings with the same blazing yet calm and steady fire."

Linda Kennedy, teacher, hypnotist, volunteer coordinator with The Visiting Nurses

"Spirit is an open window to our soul as well as a mirrored reflection of our character.

"Only Spirit knows the truth.

"When Spirit opens the character window of your soul, what will it behold: spiritual beauty and truth that will live on eternally, or the ashes of a crumbled façade to be swept away and forgotten in time?"

Betty Kibler, administrative assistant to the author

"Maybe Spirit is what one wants it to be: the innocence of a child, songs of nightingales, crashing waves, thunder, resonance of raindrops, flutter of wings, a gust of wind, a rainbow, a smile of love.

"Spirit is personal, not empirical. The only answer is to serve man. And like charity, service of man begins at home. Serve your family and friends; serve those less fortunate in your community. Keep it simple, keep it whole. Maybe that is Spirit."

Vijay S. Kothare, journalist, author

LORETTA LaROCHE

Loretta LaRoche believes that no stress is so serious you cannot laugh at it. And, she reminds us, it is time to put stress in perspective and stop treating a broken fax machine with the same grief and turmoil as a death in the family. Spirit, to her, is a great sense of humor.

"I believe in a collaborative model of stress, sort of a conspiracy of *'Isn't this funny?'*" says the author of *Relax—You May Only Have a Few Minutes Left*. "Let's look at this together. Aren't we absurd? If you reverse the word *stressed*, you have *desserts*. People will ask, where's the 'desserts' in my child being abducted or in having cancer? But if you can get to the reframing of *what can I do with my life after I found out this awful thing*, you have the brilliance of a Victor Frankel who says that we can look at suffering as a way to gain insight into our lives and to help mankind."

Humor guided LaRoche through a challenging childhood and a dismal divorce, eventually leading her to a career in teaching people how to have a little fun with their stress.

"I think I've always been funny," she says. "I just have a natural instinct to see the absurdity in the human condition. I've had that from birth. I was a breech birth; once you come out backwards you are never the same. The whole dynamic is, sort of, to laugh at the world."

Today she enjoys a healthy relationship with her second husband, her grown children, and her grandchildren. Her childhood, though, was not what most child psychologists would call fun.

"There was a lot of dysfunction. When I was seven, my mother remarried, to a man who had quite a lot of rage, and that created a whole different dynamic for me. So my humor kicked in. I started to elicit humor from the pain. I would go to school and make fun of the arguments they had. It helped me with pain; it helped me with pleasure. I got panic attacks and I would act them out, making fun of myself."

She survived, got married, had three children, then was faced with another big challenge: Her marriage of 16 years came to a halt. She was single, careerless, and raising three children—9, 13, and 16 years of age—solo.

"My humor helped me to earn a living because when I got divorced I had basically no job skills. I had a college degree, but what good was that? So I went back to school and majored in dance therapy because I just love movement. I started combining all my skills, by teaching exercise to music, as well as meditation and yoga, when no one else was doing it. I hooked up with someone who was doing energy-field work. She and I put together sort of a company to do wellness training for nurses and medical people. That was 25 years ago."

A book by the late Norman Cousins about finding the humor in illness, as well as the prodding of a friend, inspired her to build into a career her ability to make herself and others laugh. Her friend encouraged her to do a humor workshop. "I was a skeptic at that time. But I put it together: a day-long program where we played musical chairs, colored, sang. I told a lot of funny stories to a group of nurses. We called it *Humor in Healing.*"

Spirit was clearly guiding her, whispering one-liners in her ear. Before she knew it, she was hired to visit hospitals, and hob-nobbing with Patch Adams and Bernie Siegel. "It was like I found my place in life. I became my work, my work became me," she recalls.

Then PBS caught the spirit and decided to try a never-before-dared series of funny programs: *The Joy of Stress, Humor Your Stress,* and *How Serious Is This?* The programs have been shown around the world, and in hospitals and Alzheimer's units.

"People think it's 'just' laughter, but it's not. It's a model for maintaining well-being. If you are not laughing, you are depressed. A long-term withdrawal from laughter means you are clinically depressed. Each of us has the possibility of reducing anger and violence in the world by lightening up. Lightening up the spirit. Elevating it. And laughter is one of the ways of elevating the spirit."

What is Spirit? "Laughter is Spirit," she says. "Without it, you sort of have a black aura. If you look at any of the really evolved spiritual leaders in the world, they are always laughing. The Dalai Lama always has a smile on his face. He is very playful and full of laughter. So laughter has an energy, doesn't it? It sort of has a ripple effect that encompasses and embraces people. I think humor and love are very much like this. And they are very contagious."

"Spirit/soul is the quality of the individual's inner life or existence. Spirit predetermines a person's most important decisions, behavior, and communication with the world; thus, it is conveyed to the exterior and the future even in the social sense, not to mention the religious one.

"Some might believe that the manifestations of a light, creative, compassionate, and all-loving spirit in people—since such occur—is the proof of the Holy Spirit and the means of its existence. Others may say that the idea of the Holy Spirit is just the sublimation, extrapolation, and designation of the good characteristics found in people, which is praise to an acknowledged phenomenon. (This is the distinction between believer and agnostic.)

"The soul, which relies upon the heart and embraces the whole intellect, is open; therefore, it is greater than the individual, and at the same time the soul manifests itself as the pillar of one's existence."

Vytautas Landsbergis, former president of Lithuania, chairman of the Parliament

Peter Max "Flower Blossom Lady, Version II" 1993, 48″ x 60″, acrylic on canvas

"Spirit is in every brush stroke,
tireless and forceful;
Spirit is color, lots of color,
spontaneously coming out of my
own being"

Alexandra Nechita

"Spirit is one's Soul, the very heart of a human creation. It lives forever even when the body is gone and within each precious soul is a God-shaped vacuum. If you keep God from His rightful place in your life, the soul is incomplete and empty; but when God is invited to fill the vacuum, inexpressible peace and completeness will preside within."

Henri Landwirth, founder of Give Kids the World; concentration camp survivor

"Spirit is the creative life force that animates and directs our physical body. We are all innately spiritual. There is really no need to seek it. The inherent nature of our lives allows its expression if we do not impede it... Spirit is manifested through our creativity. It can be generated from our light and darkness. The force of Spirit is universal, yet directed by our own personal expression. Each vessel determines its use."

Dr. Andrew Lange, naturopathic physician

"While we are still living, God talks with us through our Spirit. The Spirit of God gives us strength."

Eric Langston, age 9

"Spirit is the fingerprint of your existence—no two are alike. Your Spirit defines who you are as an individual and what you are capable of achieving. No circumstances or external forces can change your Spirit or its potential for greatness."

Sarah Laursen, 18-year-old student-intern in the Asian antiques business

"What is Spirit? Spirit is the soul of the Institution, the Corporation, the Team, the Ensemble, and last but most important, the Individual. Spirit is the essence of an individual's being—it reflects on their action, their words, and their presence. It is with us in life, and it is present after death. It embodies the way we are remembered."

Thomas F. Leahy, dean of the School of Journalism at Queens College

TOMMY LASORDA

Tommy Lasorda grew up in a low-income family to Italian immigrant parents. He was one of five boys. At the age of 17 he headed from his home in Pennsylvania for a $100-a-week job in baseball. He was terrified, having never been more than 15 miles from home before. He says his father's inspiration carried him through, leading him to become one of the longest-lasting and most loved managers in baseball—and one of a select fraternity of managers who have been inducted into the Baseball Hall of Fame.

"The things that we possessed in our family were love, faith in God, and the ability to be whatever you wanted to be," Lasorda remembers. "My father, speaking in his broken English, probably taught me more about the philosophy of life than anyone else I've ever met—and I've met presidents, politicians, top people in the entertainment field, top people in industry."

He recalls his dad as a man of great spirit. He drove a truck in a stone quarry and was a dedicated family man who never missed a day at work. He taught his sons that obligation, commitment, and responsibility to the family was next to God. He weathered cold Pennsylvania winters and constant inhalation of rock particles, which Lasorda feels contributed to his death from lung cancer at 67. Lasorda feels his father's spirit living on.

"My dad used to say to me, 'Don't you ever give up! Don't you ever lose faith in God—if you have faith, he'll never let you down.' If I was disappointed or wasn't doing well, and I called him up, he would tell me to never talk about quitting—that nobody quits in our family. And those were the driving forces with me.

"When I started out in professional baseball at 17, I didn't know where I was going to wind up. I didn't have the ability that many other players had. The thing that kept me going was the fear of failing. The urge to succeed was the predominant thing in my mind; it's the thing that kept me going when I would walk out on the mound. What I lacked in ability, I made up for in desire, determination, and will to win. I did not want to return home a failure."

What was imparted to him by his father, he passed along to his team as manager of the Los Angeles Dodgers—an organization he has been with for 50 years. "My father used to say: 'You five boys must love each other, and you must do everything you can to help each other. If you get together on one end of a rope and pull together, you could pull a half a town with you; but if two get on one end of the rope and three on the other end, you can pull all day long and all you do is pull against each other.' I used that with my team of 25 players, a manager, and coaching staff, to inspire team spirit. I have to say, whatever success I achieved is only because of the contributions of my players."

What is Spirit? "It is the drive within you that will allow you to reach the level of success you want. But it is not just Spirit alone that carries you through life—it's got to include determination, the will to make it, to pay the price. They are all wrapped up into Spirit. There is only one route to success in life, and that is through the avenue of hard work.

"My father would say Spirit is something that is in your heart, that makes you want to go ahead. It is the feeling of believing that you can achieve anything you want. *Spirit* is also a very religious word; you have to have Spirit to love God. You have to have Spirit to love your family, to be able to do the things that you truly enjoy doing.

"I am a very fortunate man," Lasorda says. "Spirit is present every day of my life. The spirit of my family, the spirit of the organization I represent, the spirit of living in the greatest country in the world, the spirit that takes me to wherever I go in a way that allows me to do something to help other people. I always try to impart to young people that if you don't have that word, *spirit,* you'll never make it. You need it in order to make it in life."

◇ ◇

"Spirit is the part of me that is a conduit for a greater energy, a life force, that is defined as vibrantly loving, and living in peace, compassion, power, wisdom, and so much gratitude for life itself."

Helene Levin, inspirational and motivational teacher, spiritual therapist

"Spirit is the Divine and life-activating principle or vital essence, symbolizing the part of our soul that bestows the ability to experience independent thought. It is associated with thought, will, and cognition."

Gurunam Joseph Levry, life management consultant, industrial engineer

"Spirit *is*. It is not anything or anybody. It just is. The source of everything. The intelligence of life. The seed of our awakening. The eyes of our vision. The breath of our inspiration. The arrow that guides our passage. The sanctuary at the end of our journey, and the magic that starts it all over again."

Jacob Liberman, O.D., Ph.D., optometrist, author, public speaker, scientist

"Spirit is that quality of humankind that lets us soar with the eagles and walk with the sparrows. To reach for a star and to dream dreams. To see love in the most forlorn, and hope in a wayside puddle."

J. Thomas Liston, real estate broker

"Spirit Is the Breath of God. Every thing and every body from all dimensions that ever were or ever will be are all linked into the Spirit of God's one eternal breath."

Gregory Lording, film producer

"What is Spirit? Close your eyes and concentrate on the inner sky. Drop your bucket to the bottom of your well and drink deeply from the cool waters of peace.

"Open your eyes and see that same significance in all people and in the sparkle of those perceptions by which we weave the tapestry of our world."

Malcolm MacDonald, healer and teacher of Chinese herbal arts

"Spirit is the pure essence of creation. Infinite and eternal."

Phyllis Maisel, awareness consultant

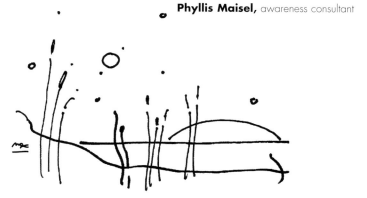

LEO

"Spirit is the love of God," says Leo, a man who does not like to give out his last name. Once homeless and addicted to alcohol, Leo is now something of a goodwill ambassador in his midtown Manhattan neighborhood.

Leo has a big heart, a sweet nature. He loves to read and to share his library of books with neighbors. The women in his neighborhood love him and often stop to chat on the way to the market. Seeing him today, it is hard to believe he used to spend his days dazed, drunk, and disconnected from the community. He is sure that Spirit lifted him to a higher ground and helped him get his life together.

Leo's big wake-up call to Spirit came when his longtime street associate was violently killed one night. "That scared me," Leo says. "At the time, I was drinking and living on the streets." Something guided him into a local church and inspired him to read the Bible; as he did, an energy other than his own seemed to be with him.

"I sat in the church with a pint of vodka in my pocket, and I read the Bible for an hour and a half," he recalls. "I'm not sure exactly what happened. I walked out of that church—I was going to take a drink— but I got as far as the gutter and emptied the bottle. Just poured it out. It has been over five years since I've had a drink."

He never went back to drinking. Instead, he moved forward with his life and found a program that would give him a room of his own— a place to stay and a place to keep his books. Now, when neighbors see

Peter Max "Angel Series, Version III, #2" 1989, 20″ x 16″, acrylic on canvas

"When I saw Nelson Mandela walk out of jail
with no hatred and no bitterness,
I realized he had authentic Spirit"

Dick Gregory

him on the street, they are greeted by a warm and loving presence. There is a twinkle in his eye that could best be described as Spirit.

"Spirit is so undefinable and almost diaphanous. I've seen it, though. I've seen it in the bright eyes of my puppy as she faces new experiences daily; in an enthusiastic child standing before a class delivering a lesson; in an Olympian skiing down a huge slope in blinding snow. It's an inner force, an inner drive. It's heroism and bravery without reward. It's spontaneous. It's Rosa Parks refusing to go to the back of the bus. It's the man who pulls off his jacket to jump into the freezing river to rescue a drowning person. It's Patrick Kennedy with his prosthetic leg running a marathon. It's the people who go about their daily lives in a wheelchair or are led to work by a guide dog. Spirit is innate. It can't be taught or learned. I've seen it in the eyes of my own husband, refusing to buckle down to injustice. It's our soul. I don't think everybody has it, though. It's a gift from God."

Miriam Mandell, self-employed retailer, helper to the homeless

"To answer *What is Spirit?* I first raised the question, *Who am I?* And began to realize that I was the living being sitting quietly behind my eyes in the form of a point of light, starlike. But I know and feel that it doesn't stop there, because there's a recording in the living being, a point of light in the form of a star, a recording that spanned many lifetimes. The recording of that which was true, the duty, the Goddess, and a recording when I left that role and played another; as a result I am here looking within the Spirit, the living being, and I realized I'm one of the actors in an eternal cycle, and right now I choose to reconnect with the Supreme Being, so I can rekindle the Goddess in me."

B.K. (Brahma Kumaris) Jenna Maragh, spiritual teacher

"Spirit is that easy feeling between two strangers who have just met or spoken, and words are no longer necessary. The eye contact mirrors the heart and the feelings within. Time, distance, age, race, sexuality are all gone—they have no relevance. The sense of one that exists between two people who are strangers, but still know all they need to know—the eyes being the windows into the soul and the mirror of the heart. Spirit is the comfort and ease that exists between people who would rather give than receive."

Maxfield B. Matthewson, M.D., physician in the fertility field

"My Spirit comes to me when I meditate. I sit peacefully and breathe. Sometimes my Spirit sounds like the wind in the trees, as I breathe, or an ocean breaking on the beach. As I listen to my breathing, I let my thoughts come naturally, and whatever comes to me I feel is my Spirit telling my innermost thoughts. When I want a vision or a decision about something, I count on my meditation to guide me. It works every time, and I have made some really important decisions this way. Then I journalize these thoughts to give myself reference for the future. That is Spirit in action."

Kathleen McConnell, safety professional for an air fleet

"There is a Spirit that guides me, a light that shines for me. In 1973, when the Mets won the Nationals in Canada, coming from way behind, I came up with the slogan 'You Gotta Believe.' That slogan came out of threads of frustration one day—in front of the media—and turned into a headline. Over the years I have thought about it tremendously. It really is directly associated with Spirit. To me, trust is the foundation, the cornerstone, of Spirit. The wider you can reach, the further out you go in your life; then the more people you can develop relationships with and trust—just as they trust you. Then the level of Spirit goes higher."

Tug McGraw, former New York Mets and Philadelphia Phillies pitcher, motivational speaker

"Spirit is life. Spirit is inside us. Spirit is all around us."

Justin McNamara, age 7

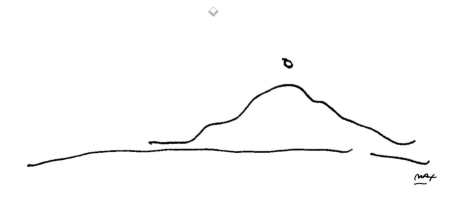

PETER MAX

Peter Max's imagery, vibrant colors, and bold graphics are a hugely recognizable part of our culture. But Max has brought more than legendary art to this country—he has brought an important infusion of Spirit and spiritual awareness.

It was Max who introduced America to Swami Satchidananda, one of the most beloved and respected spiritual teachers of our time. The founder of Integral Yoga, Swami Satchidananda's core philosophy is "Paths are many, but truth is one." He was one of the first gurus to embrace all faiths, encourage communion with the Divine, and suggest that it matters not how we walk the path to Spirit—as long as we walk it.

Max's early childhood in China prepared him for the path he would eventually follow. "I lived there for ten years amid the Oriental philosophy, the mystics, the holy people, and the Buddhist temples and the monks, never knowing that kids grew up differently in other parts of the world," he says.

He was able to rekindle that spiritual attitude in the '60s because "the hippie generation had a very big interest in spirituality." Inspired, he tried to access a deeper meaning of life through his art. In 1966 he was working three days and nights on a huge collage of the universe, when he had an epiphany that would completely change his life.

"I was creating this collage of all the different aspects the universe was made from," he recalls. "I had borrowed a ladder to climb up to the ceiling so I could look down at the collage to see if I could get insight into what the universe was about. When I got to the top of the ladder and looked down, all I saw was my collage, not the answer I was looking for. I was so heartbroken and disappointed that I reached out to God, looking for help; a vision appeared of a holy man with a white beard. He seemed to say, 'Everything is okay. Just relax.'

"At that moment the phone rang. It was a young filmmaker calling me from Paris to tell me that he wanted me to fly the next day to meet him there because he was making a movie about the meaning of life." Max flew to Paris. This was Spirit's way of helping him make the connection with one who would become—and still is—his spiritual teacher and guide.

"So I met with the filmmaker and he tells me that 'the Swami' will be joining us," Max says. "The elevator doors of the hotel opened, and out came this tall, very beautiful figure, with long black curly hair and an orange robe. It was Swami Satchidananda. I was highly touched by him, by the look in his beautiful eyes. It is the most amazing thing when you are with a real holy man and you look in his eyes. There is nobody there except an ocean of love. You have to blink after a while—it is just too much."

The meeting with Swami Satchidananda restimulated Max's childhood memory. The Swami took him under his spiritual wing and taught him the discipline of yoga. Max became a devoted student and invited the Swami to come to America.

Max put together a gathering of his most conscious and health-minded friends to hear the Swami speak. "We all realized he was the embodiment of what we were all searching for in the '60s—a holy man, teacher, and a master of an ancient transmission has passed from generation to generation for 4,000 years. It was something very, very holy, and we wanted to have it, own it, swim in it, be part of it. So Max and his friends raised money to start a center, and since 1966, Integral Yoga Centers have opened across the country, including the 100-acre ashram in West Virginia, where the Swami lives.

What is Spirit? "Spirit is the inner self that is you. Some people have a spunky Spirit, some have a spiritual Spirit, and some a teaching Spirit. Spirit is the essence in you that is the driver behind the body."

"Spirit is a state of mind that frees us to be in harmony with all elements of the universe. It is not limited by the five senses; rather, it transcends them so that we have a clearer view and understanding of our relation to God, nature, and all living creatures."

Harold Miller, M.D., retired doctor

Jim Nabors

Jim Nabors is widely recognized for his portrayal of the lovable Gomer Pyle television character and for his surprisingly deep and rich voice in countless recordings. The world also remembers his most desperate hours in the early 1990s when he needed a liver transplant to live. Just as Nabors's faith and optimism were recounted in the tabloids back then, his reflections today remain constant: He always knew that Spirit was with him. He never really believed he would die, even though his body was, by all accounts, dying.

"They had given me about two months to live unless I could find a transplant—and I was going pretty fast," he says. "When they finally found my organ, I probably had less than a week left. I could feel things closing down on me."

The availability of a compatible liver truly did come at the 11th hour, yet Nabors didn't see this as sudden divine intervention. "I felt that Spirit was always there. My relationship with God has always been intact. I've never really felt I was without that in my life. Spirit was always very apparent, always with me. So I never really thought about it."

What did concern him was the unknown aspect of Spirit, as it existed on the other side. "I was apprehensive because none of us know how it is to cross over," he admits. "Most people put their mortality way down the road. It is not there until suddenly you are confronted with it and you say, 'Oh … hello?' I came to feel it was just another undertaking I had with life that you experience."

Spirit came to Nabors in his weakened state, in the form of outpouring love from fans. "I received 200,000 or more letters and prayers from people all over the country. People in different churches would send me huge things with all their names on it and would pray for me. I have to tell you, it makes you feel not worthy. I'd had such a rich life—a wonderful family, marvelous friends, and a great career. I felt almost presumptuous asking God for any more time if he was ready for me then."

Although Nabors's experience didn't make him trust in Spirit more than before, it did teach him that time, energy, and health are precious gifts to be used wisely. "The thing that bothered me most was the amount of time you waste worrying about inconsequential things that just do not mean a thing in your life. I realized that when the penny finally drops, the only thing you take with you is who you are. It is the culmination. If you were evil or bad, that is what you are going to take over. And if you have been a fairly decent person, that is what you take."

It might be said that Spirit led Nabors back into the recording studio to express some of what he feels. "I was very fortunate and very blessed," he says of his illness and his healing. "The whole experience was a total blessing to me. I'm just happy to be here. That is one of the reasons I went to Nashville to do a spiritual album. I had not recorded in about 20 years, but suddenly I wanted a way of letting people know how I really felt about things. And music to me is the best way to convey that."

What is Spirit? "Spirit is that indefinable thing within yourself. You know that God exists within you, and through him all things are possible. I knew that, especially when I was so ill."

◇ ◇

"I think Spirit is the basis of our life. It guides us toward our experience. I had lots of difficulties in my life, but I am happy. I think it is because of my Spirit that I am happy and surviving."

Ven Lobsang Thinley, Tibetan monk

"The qualified achievements and negative abandonments are only available for those who have Spirit, so *I think Spirit is the essential nature of living beings.*

"Because of the existence of Spirit, we have the ability to create happiness and harmony within ourselves and the community. Also, we have the ability to solve mental and physical problems by applying antidotes to the causes of the problems or afflicted emotions and bad actions. One can achieve higher qualities of happiness and mental peace by practicing good behaviors, universal love, and compassion; with wisdom, we can realize truth and strengthen our physical and mental power. That's the reason we develop spiritual practices.

"On the negative side, when we do not develop these practices, we lose our spiritual power. Then problems start, or we experience physical, mental, and spiritual sufferings. So when something bad happens, we talk about bad Spirit. *Every good and bad quality, and happy and unhappy feeling we are possessing and experiencing all come to exist because of our spirit.* Spirit allows for their existence. It makes them flexible as well. So there is a way we can create happiness and solve problems in individuals and communities by sharing thoughts and communicating. These are all because of our Spirit."

Ven Ngawang Tashi Bapu, Tibetan monk

"I think Spirit is the continuation of consciousness, which is also the temporary basis of predisposition. Because continuation of consciousness has both good and bad effects, we experience both happiness and suffering in our life.

"As we know, when we work with compassionate intention, even if it is hard work, our efforts do not feel difficult."

Ven Khenrab Penpa, Tibetan monk

"I think that the mental continuum that serves as a basis for our good and bad predisposition is Spirit.

"We experience happiness because of the gentleness of our mental continuum, and because of its badness we experience suffering. For instance, you can see various great beings—how strong are they? I think that, because of the gentleness of their mental continuum or their good Spirit, they have great strength. I think our life force or life experience depends on it."

Ven Tenzin Kunsal (Ahten), Tibetan monk

"I think Spirit is the basis of mental power and physical energy. Living strengthens our mental power and physical energy. Without Spirit we cannot survive, so I think it's an essential power of life. Because of our Spirit we sometimes experience extraordinary happiness in our life, even when it seems impossible with our physical energy and mental power."

Ven Thupten Gyaltsen, Tibetan monk

"I think Spirit is follower of consciousness that creates the relation of mental power and physical energy and causes them to act or manifest. It indirectly creates all the experience of our life. It only abides those who have consciousness and physical energy. Without Spirit, we cannot solve problems or bring happiness in our experiences."

Ven Yeshi Jampel, Tibetan monk

◇

"I think Spirit is a formless and nonconscious power that makes us survive.

"Very unusual experiences can happen in life because of spiritual power. I have an interesting story about it. Once, because of a famine, people were dying. A wise man did not want to upset his children by saying that they didn't have food to eat, so he filled up a bag full of dust and tied it to a high beam that his children could not reach. He told the children that their food was inside. The children were waiting for it, and they lived without food for a long time. Unfortunately, one day, the bag fell down and the children discovered that it was just dust inside the bag. Soon after that, they all died. I think that's because of Spirit. From this story you can learn that the mental has power over the physical. I think all of our life experiences depend upon that power or Spirit."

Palden Thinley, Tibetan monk

◇

"Spirit is said to be 'a special power that increases and strengthens the virtuous and nonvirtuous behaviors and actions.' Generally, the happy and unhappy, good and bad, of our life all arise from good and bad actions of our past life and this one. And Spirit supports the good and bad in our life experience. That is how it relates to me and my life experience.

"For instance, when I became a monk I didn't know the benefits of it. I was too young. But I did it, and now I am very happy with who I am. I believe that happened because of good action from my last life, and Spirit supports goodness.

"I think there are many things happening in our life, more than we expect. I think that is because of Spirit."

Ngawang Phendey, Tibetan monk

These Buddhist monks of the Drepung Loseling Monastery in Southern India unanimously agree that their greatest accomplishment is their spiritual practice, and they all graciously share their healing chants, energy, and smiles with all who are open to receiving such blessings.

"When I was growing up, my mother always told me, 'Don't forget who you are, and make yourself strong.' She wasn't talking about my physical self. She was talking about the essence of my soul. It has had a huge effect on my life. When I've lost my way, my mother's words have put me back in touch with my higher self and healed my attitude and thoughts, which healed me."

Patricia Myura, president of a charitable foundation

"Spirit is the force that turns life into living. It is what animates, infuses, charges, pushes, excites, and makes powerful all of human function. It starts as biology—the way we have been wired to bring anything to attention and consciousness once it triggers an emotion.

"To the extent that we are willing to resonate with the Spirit of another person, the two of us are able to achieve emotional intimacy. To the extent that we are able to link our Spirits to form a group or a congregation or a community of any sort, it allows us to maximize our ability to join as part of a whole. Conscious of our own Spirit, accepting the Spirit of another, able to welcome the Spirit of our community, we live in both inner and outer harmony. Dispirited, shorn of our ability to locate and stay with excitement and joy, we shrivel from ourselves and from whoever might become our intimate other and form our community. The life of the Spirit is life itself."

Don Nathanson, M.D., renowned psychiatrist and author

"Spirit is in every brush stroke, tireless and forceful; Spirit is color, lots of color, spontaneously coming out of my own being. It is the core of my journey on canvas. My colors are happy—colors are me…a very happy me."

Alexandra Nechita, world-famous teenage artist

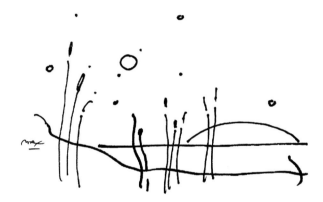

Adrian Paul

While starring in the *Highlander* television series, actor Adrian Paul discovered the power of celebrity—and the extraordinary influence celebrities have on youngsters. Since children tend to place stars on a pedestal and be guided by whatever information is imparted to them, Paul came up with an idea to make larger-than-life heroes and heroines accessible to children as positive role models. Adrian's fan club donates a certain portion of proceeds to charity. His fan club is celebrating its sixth year in operation and supports a wide variety of charities. In 1998, Adrian expanded his charity work with children and created the PEACE Fund, which stands for Protect, Educate, and Aid Children Everywhere.

"What really set me on this path was contact with children," Paul says. "I would be swamped by kids in Paris and other places I would go. I'd watch their reactions and found it surprising because I am just a normal guy. I realized that through media I was able to reach out to a lot of people."

In the role of Duncan McCloud, Paul played an "Immortal" and spent his days trying to avoid getting his head cut off—the only way to end an Immortal's life. His character was highly intuitive, led by Spirit in his ability to sense adversaries and lurking danger, and he was mighty with a sword. He was also compassionate, loving, and gentle.

"Everyone brings a part of themselves to whatever character they play," he says. "Yet *Highlander* actually made me grow as a human being."

Being the object of public attention was daunting to Paul at first, yet he began to appreciate that his character—and characters played by many actors—provide role models for children. He envisioned a program in which individuals from different walks of fame could be matched with youngsters with life challenges and issues to share inspiration or a story from their own lives.

"Because of *Highlander,* there were a lot of people who kept coming up and telling me, 'I have changed my life because of you.' That stunned me. Whether it was the spiritual, historical, or the physical level of the series, people found something that could help them better their lives."

Paul explains, "Many celebrities do events and charities that they don't feel connected to, but they want to help." Rechanneling that celebrity power into brief, one-on-one meetings with children could, he felt, literally turn lives around.

The aim of the PEACE Fund is to set up programs for children who are financially disadvantaged or come from backgrounds where they cannot help themselves, and to offer brief conversations with a favorite celebrity. "Whether it is a sports, television, or film celebrity, someone who is a celebrity in a child's eyes can make a great impact if they get close and talk with that child," Paul says.

What is Spirit? "I think it is finding peace in your life. Usually happiness is connected with material things these days, and I don't think that's what it's about. Everybody's peace is different. Mine, obviously, is something that I am searching to achieve; giving back and working

Peter Max "Heart, Version V, # 1" 1997, 28˝ x 22˝, acrylic on canvas

"Spirit is the essence in you
that is the driver behind the body"

Peter Max

with children will give me my own peace. I have always believed in a higher Spirit, a higher being." Paul says that Spirit has led him on a journey of his own awareness and led him on a mission of utilizing celebrity to serve others. "I realized I was given the ability to touch people through a television screen," Paul says. "For many years I felt there was 'something else' I was supposed to achieve, something for my own Spirit, but I wasn't quite sure what it was. I suddenly felt that doing something for the benefit of children was something I needed to do with my life. I would like to be known as somebody who cares for other people, who is trying to improve the quality of life around myself and others."

◇ ◇

"I sense Spirit in all living things, taking care not to leave out the animals, plants, water, and rocks. You can see the Spirit of the forest when you lie down under its canopy. Look for the sky's thousand faces outlined by the overlapping leaves. Spirit is sensuous and rising, like roots pushing upward for life, on the side of the pavement; it is resilient like the weathered faces of people of the sun. It's something of ourselves but beyond ourselves and connected in a web of life."

Nguyenvu Nguyen, escaped from Vietnam; went on to medical school

"I believe Spirit is an energetic intelligence that may be accessed through quieting the mind in meditation, the journeys of Shamanism, directed prayer, and dreaming. Spirit is absolute truth."

Susan Obermeyer, artist, creator of shamanic paintings, writer

"In my limited understanding, Spirit is that which connects us all. The vision of unity, consciousness, and oneness is found in virtually all cultures and all religions. Spirit or God or the Self is described as omniscient, omnipresent, and omnipotent. As described in the Old Testament, 'The Lord is One.' If Spirit is everywhere, One, then we are not separate from Spirit."

Dean Ornish, M.D., author; director of the Preventative Medicine Research Institute

"When my dance company tours, we travel all over the world and into some very small communities where exposure to the performing arts does not happen often. In some of these places, I am asked to work with kids with special needs, like the hearing-impaired kids we worked with on our last tour of Brazil. I have to say that it is quite magical to watch these kids go from apprehension to complete abandon and joy. That is Spirit.

"Nothing expresses Spirit like raw, uninhibited movement from the soul. I leave these kids feeling fortunate that they have allowed me to take part in the Spirit of their life."

David Parsons, artistic director of the David Parsons Dance Company

"Spirit is energy and enthusiasm about living a creative life, whether you are a choreographer, a painter, a business person, or involved in religion. It's all about harnessing, gathering, binding, and maintaining this energy, which is the life force. Spirit is the kind of energy you give to an inanimate object, so that it becomes something that can attract the eye of an audience and actually give *them* some spirit. I don't go to church but I'm quite faithful to every sunset that I can catch. I find Spirit in nature.

"The more Spirit you have, the more ability you have to dream in the daytime, which allows you to see several levels to situations. We need this kind of creative Spirit-energy around us; then we can begin to see how we can operate in it, swim in it, and drown in it."

Moses Pendleton, dancer, director, avid photographer, choreographer

"In my business you have to be full of Spirit to be good. If not, you are not going to be able to perform. Spirit is the place you create from. For me to create I have to be very spiritual. You have to put yourself in a kind of mood, so for me it's very spiritual. Of course, you can be inspired by anything, but when I want to create great food I want to feel something about what I'm creating. I would say that is Spirit—something to make you to do things differently than you do every day of your life."

George Perrier, owner of Le Bec-Fin and Brasserie Perrier restaurants in Philadelphia

"For me, Spirit is the essence of who we are. It is the tiny point of life located behind my forehead that is my true and higher self. It cannot be seen with the eye, but once we begin to get in touch with our soul, or Spirit, we know it exists. It begins with this awareness that we truly are Spirit and not material or physical. Once this awakening takes place, everything in our life changes.

"This Spirit consciousness, or soul consciousness, leads us to a new and transformed life. We begin to see that we are here to love and spread light, and to teach others how to live this way also. My aim in life now is to live more in soul or Spirit consciousness so that I can connect in this loving and caring way with everyone I meet and know."

Meredith Porte, television producer

KENNETH REIGHTLER JR.

In his eight years as a NASA astronaut, Kenneth Reightler Jr., flew two space shuttle missions, logged over 327 hours in space, and orbited Earth 212 times. He piloted the first joint U.S.–Russian space shuttle mission.

Now a vice president and program manager for Lockheed Martin Space Mission Systems, he is responsible for science, engineering, analysis, and test operation, and works with more than 2,300 people—in contrast to the 100 or so astronauts who were in the space program in the early '90s. He was also a consultant for the movie *Apollo 13*. "I had a role in helping to get those guys to the point where they could actually talk and act like astronauts," he says. "And I showed Tom Hanks how to land a space shuttle."

Going into space changed Reightler's world view and showed him the vastness of Spirit. From out there, there are no boundaries, no dividing lines. "Being in space showed me there are very few limits," he says. "Only the ones we choose to place on ourselves.

"The trip into space only takes eight minutes," he says. "You're going from zero to over 17,000 miles per hour in eight minutes. But once you get into space, everything slows down. I vividly remember releasing my seatbelt, floating out of my seat, coming up to the windows, and looking at Earth for the first time. It was an unbelievable sight."

The first thing that struck him was that he was unprepared for the beauty before him. "There was the realization that this was so much more beautiful than anything I had either imagined or seen before," he says. "Looking down at Earth, you get the impression that all of this did not happen by accident. There had to be some plan; this is all just too incredibly beautiful and complex for everything to just kind of happen by accident.

"From the perspective of the human spirit, what spoke to me is that Earth is not as big as we imagine it, and it is much more connected. When you look at a map in an atlas, the countries are separated with different colors. When you look at Earth from space, it is all neutral colors, all one planet. You get a sense that people are more connected than we think; you get a sense of how close things are.

"Coming across Canada and looking out the front windows of the shuttle, I remember taking in the whole Gulf Coast view of the United States, then looking out the right window and seeing the West Coast, and seeing the East Coast out the left—I got a connection that this is a very small country. It made me think that people really are not all that different," he recalls.

What is Spirit? "There are a lot of aspects of human spirit that are brought out in space exploration. A facet of the human spirit is the concept of exploration; that spirit very clearly is a great motivator for why we feel this great need to explore. It is not just the spirit of adventure, or just something that a few brave souls want to do. It is something inside all of us. Whether it is exploring in your own backyard or in exotic locales, it's a life-changing experience. It changes our perspective on the world, on ourselves, on our environment. It is something that everyone, in some way, needs to do. Astronauts have that spirit of exploration in common. There is also spirit in terms of team work, cooperation, and working with other people—that is part of the human spirit and an essential ingredient in a space shuttle crew or space station crew."

"Spirit is something inside you that tells you to do right, not wrong. Spirit urges you to do good, and the urge that Spirit sends is so strong. Spirit is a voice from inside you that is always there when you are sad. Spirit is your best friend, your buddy, a friend that was made just for you. Spirit is always there for you—a friend that is there through and through."

Andi Potamkin, age 10

"Spirit is the intangible yet undeniable force of life that courses through our bodies and minds. It presents itself on many levels of our conscious and subconscious selves. Spirit is the inspiration we feel to help those in need and to assist the growth in ourselves, our loved ones, and those we've never even met. It is what tickles us when we recognize humor, and brings tears of joy or sadness when we hear a particular song. It is the strength that wells up in us to push forth when we feel we have no more to give. It is love, it is light, it is our connection with every other soul on the earth and beyond, and it is our bond with God."

Claudia Potamkin, broadcast announcer, journalist, race car driver

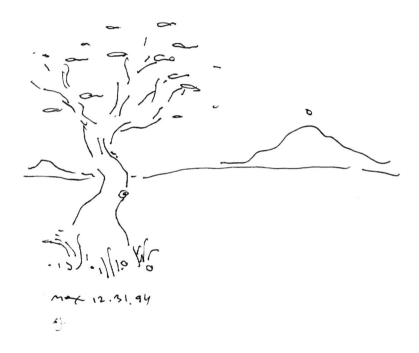

Max 12.31.94

127

"Spirit is the home within us. It is in all of us; yet each of us has our own special meaning for it. That is the paradox of Spirit. It is unique and universal all at once."

Melissa Potamkin-Ganzi, marriage and family therapist

"I took a course to get a master's degree in applied psychology. I kept hearing about Spirit and I wasn't sure what it was. It was like 'The Emperor's Clothes'—no one asked what it was—we were all just supposed to know. So I asked the question and received a different answer from each person. I am still trying to find my answer, but it is elusive. Spirit is where we all come from, and where we all return to. Spirit is what makes us each unique, and yet it makes us all one. We are each born knowing what Spirit is, and yet we each spend a lifetime trying to figure it out."

Robert Potamkin, successful entrepreneur and attorney

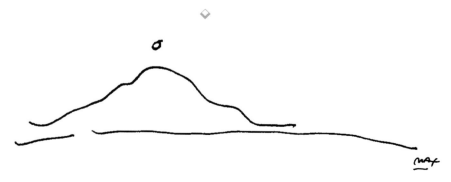

"The spirit of the scientist is the path to discovery—that pushing and shoving and moving. Spirit is the excitement of being the first person to really understand what some piece of nature is really doing, whether it's in physics, chemistry, or biology—it doesn't matter… Religion is trying to explain the unknown by some belief set, and science is all about tearing down these unknowns and figuring out what they mean—the two are like oil and water. But there are a lot of scientists who, at the end of their life, pray to God that something good will happen to them after they die."

Stanley B. Prusiner, M.D., 1997 Nobel Prize winner in medicine

"Spirit is the gift from the Creator to His Creation to become one with Him. To become one with the rain forest, one with the starving child in Afghanistan, one with the creatures of the sea, one with the animals of the forest, one with the teeming humanity of Earth, one with the forming galaxies of the Universe. Spirit is the one-breath of all that ever was, that is now, and that will be."

Virginia G. Rangnow, bookkeeper, credit manager

Bill Rossiter

When Bill Rossiter purchased sacred land in the Southwest, he had no idea that this magical place—site of an ancient Pueblo burial ground—would start him on the healing journey that would save his life. Led by Spirit to Native American ways, he would confront his own death, heal himself of terminal illness, and ultimately create richer bonds with his family, extended clan, and Great Spirit.

"Because of the effect that sacred land had on us, we became extremely interested in Native American healing," says Rossiter, once the president of a chemical company. After reading Medicine Cards, a divination system similar to Tarot but based on the healing, insight, wisdom, and warnings inherent in animal medicine, he contacted one of the authors, David Carson. Soon Carson, a medicine man, came for a visit.

"That was the beginning of the discovery of my cancer," says Rossiter. In the evening Carson did an animal card reading. "You have something inside of you that needs to be removed, and you need to do a sweat lodge ceremony to get at the source of the disease," Carson told Rossiter, who remembers, "That was the first inkling. My response was the feeling: *Listen to this.*" He went to the doctor three days later to learn he had prostate cancer. Rossiter recalls, "I had a tumor and was told it was inoperable." A second opinion confirmed it.

Rossiter called Carson to request the sweat lodge: a four-day ceremony in a tepee with heated rocks in the center. The participants sit in a circle chanting, singing, drumming, praying, and communicating. Water is poured upon the rocks to create intense steam at pivotal moments. It is an extraordinary purification physically, emotionally, and spiritually. Four of his children and his wife joined him.

Each day was devoted to a theme: "The first was a day of love. At just the right moment, the medicine man said to my family, 'Tell this man how you feel about him as if this were the last chance you had to express it.' That was powerful. The second day was a day of truth. The third was a day of strength and courage; the fourth was a day of joy and happiness. My children were there for the whole time."

"I was also taken on a shaman's journey to visit the source of my disease," Rossiter recalls. "They asked me to name my tumor. They said that if you want something to be removed, you need to talk to it and ask in a personal way if it would not suit it to go someplace else. So I named my tumor Activity." He felt that the tumor represented a lifetime of "being a businessman, instead of facing my issues with feelings," something that it was time to release.

Simultaneously, Rossiter went on conventional medication, returning to the doctor a month later. "I walked in and the doctor asked, 'How was the sweat?'" Rossiter recalls. "I said that it was the most powerful spiritual experience I'd ever had, and that I didn't think there was a tumor there anymore." His doctor examined him and could not find anything. An associate who was called in could not find anything either. They couldn't believe it. A year later, there was nothing. He stayed on conventional medicine for three and a half years.

"I changed my entire life," he laughs. "Before, I was president of Owen Chemicals in Stanford, Connecticut. Now, I've turned into a human being instead of a human doing. I have a mission in life. I do a lot of work with men and shadow. I help a lot of cancer patients. Cancer was probably one of the better things that ever happened to me."

What is Spirit? "The very essence of the sweat lodge ceremony is Spirit. You call in the directions, so the ancestors and the Great Spirit are present. You may call it Holy Spirit. My wife calls it Divine Mother, which is the feminine form of God. They are all one. What I learned, and am still learning, is that I need to preserve a space deep inside me in which I can laugh, dance, sing, and play. Then, I am filled with Spirit; I am one with the Spirit and with the universe."

❖ ❖

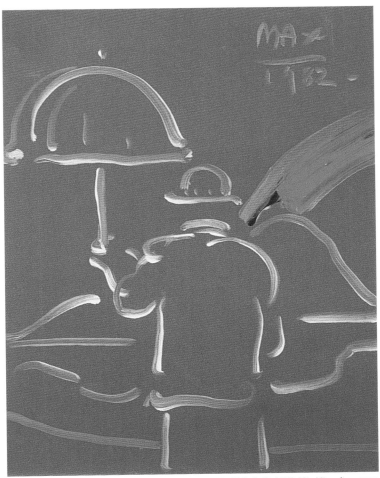

Peter Max "Umbrella Man" 1982, 20″ x 16″, acrylic on canvas

"The people I have found to be the most successful
are not necessarily the smartest people,
but the people with the most
spirit and enthusiasm"

Donald Trump

"I feel that spirituality is the foundation of all Spirit. Spirituality is God's teaching. It lives forever in one's soul and is not ego-centered. It trusts others, mends quarrels, fights for principles, does favors, appreciates nature, forgets grudges, encourages others, accepts fears, handles tragedies, and shares the love and grace of life. Spirit is the vim, vigor, time, and energy that enables a person to carry out spirituality during life."

Jack Rasmussen, retired attorney, survivor of two wars

"Spirit is the invisible vibration of wee spirits of peace, love, purity, wisdom, and bliss; it represents the best in ourselves and helps to bring out the best in others. This vibration is in all of us and cannot be purchased in any shopping mall."

Rosalyn Reich, retired professor

"To me, Spirit is the will to change things, and to do whatever is necessary to bring about these changes.

"The best example of Spirit is how everyone in Philadelphia rallied around the city at its darkest hour in 1992. Almost by force of will, people—community leaders, business leaders, and elected officials—refused to give up and, ultimately, brought the city back.

"Philadelphia is a city of neighborhoods with people who have lived here all their lives. They have a special feeling for their city—this Spirit makes Philadelphia a very special place."

Edward Rendell, mayor of Philadelphia (1991–1999)

"When I think of Spirit, I think of my mother, who got polio when she was pregnant with my sister. I think if there's any Spirit in me, it comes from my mother, who is now in a wheelchair because of her polio. When we were children she walked with sticks—and we always played with them. There was nothing she could not do. She raised five children, she worked full time, she told me she used to be a gymnast—after I got into gymnastics. She was fabulous; she was really my inspiration. There might have been a physical challenge, but I never saw it. She always did what she had to do, and she was very strong—filled with Spirit."

Cathy Rigby, two-time Olympic gymnast; actress

"Spirit is learning to be gentle. For centuries, humans have said to horses, 'You do what I tell you, or I'll hurt you.' Humans still say that to each other—still threaten, force, and intimidate. I'm convinced that my discoveries with horses also have value in the workplace, in the educational and penal systems, and in raising children. At heart, I'm saying that no one has the right to say 'you must' to an animal—or to another human. My greatest accomplishment was learning to be gentle. Without that, I would have accomplished nothing."

Monty Roberts, real-life horse whisperer; author of *The Man Who Listens to Horses*

GAYLE SAYERS

On the football field, Gayle Sayers was the embodiment of spirit and grace. As a running back for the Chicago Bears in the '60s and early '70s, he was a national hero—his performance, pure poetry in motion. He was completely devoted to football, until life threw him an incomplete pass. The story that transformed him from a young man who lived and breathed his sport to a mature person who was first and foremost a friend was eloquently told in the movie *Brian's Song*.

Sayers, who owns a chain of computer stores and devotes an extraordinary amount of time and energy to numerous charities, says the experience of going through the dying and death of his good friend and fellow teammate Brian Piccolo was an extraordinary awakening in his life. Piccolo passed away at the age of 26, in 1970, from testicular cancer.

"When I look back on that period of my life, when Brian and I started rooming together and he got sick, I think that football was Number 1, 2, and 3 in my life. Although I was married, it was football, football, football. I didn't want anything to interrupt my quest to be a good football player. And when this happened to Brian, it really made football unimportant. My only thought was, *Can he beat this terrible disease?* When he died, it taught me that we do take life for granted. It could be taken away any day.

"The experience put things back into perspective. I told myself to pay more attention to my children, love them more, love my wife more, pay more attention to my friends, do some other things—don't just think football. Just being around for that year that he suffered with his disease made me realize that there are more important things out there than just playing football."

Brian's death was the first of many endings for Sayers. "My mother died of cancer about a year and a half after Brian died. My father died of a chronic disease in between the two. Then, preparing myself to quit football came early because I had knees that could not play anymore. I grew up very quickly, because I was only 27 and I thought I could do everything; then all of a sudden I'm out of football. The realization that I could not play any longer made me grow up and find a job."

He became a success in yet another field and decided to devote much time to his family life and to charitable organizations. Married for 25 years, with three kids and one grandchild, Sayers makes his home in Chicago. His computer business is based in town, with offices in Arizona, California, Indiana, Massachusetts, Missouri, and Texas.

His passion these days is helping out with numerous charitable organizations, such as the Mark Lund Children's Home for severely handicapped children and as a board member of the Cradle Adoption Agency. "My oldest son is adopted from the Cradle. There are so many babies out there who need adoption—they are just waiting. Some of these babies will grow up to be a Martin Luther King or John Kennedy. I do a lot of work for them."

What is Spirit? "I think Spirit is being able to appreciate the things that you have and being willing to go out and help those less fortunate than you to acquire some of the things you have. Many people take having some milk for breakfast for granted. Yet a lot of people don't have milk for breakfast. So I am very happy at the level that I have achieved, but I know there are many other people out there who are not at my level. I am involved in many fund-raisers to help these people achieve more in life."

"Spirit is the combination of your heart, your mind, and your soul. Viewed through your smiles and your eyes, it is what lingers when you leave a room. Spirit is the gift we give to all those we touch. It is the part of us that lives on and on in them after we are gone."

Ellyn Golder Saft, fashion columnist

"Spirit is a metaphor for the very phenomenon of evolution."

Jonas Salk, M.D., world-renowned doctor who introduced the first successful polio vaccine

"Spirit is God's most precious gift to mankind, as it makes us unique among species. It is the energy that fuels our lives, influences our emotions, and feeds our souls, while it nurtures our experiences. Spirit is immortal and eternal."

Orlando Sanchez, project manager for a building company

"Spirit is that spark of the Divine or Cosmic Consciousness within each of us. Spirit is what gives us life; it flows through us much as gasoline flows through a car engine. A car cannot run without gasoline. But plain gasoline cannot carry you on your journey! Gasoline needs to flow into an engine, which powers the car that takes you on the journey of life. In our case, as human beings, Spirit is the gasoline, the engine is the mind, and the body of the car is the human body. Everything works only if the Spirit is there.

"Spirit is Cosmic Consciousness. It is omnipresent, omnipotent, and omniscient. Everything visible and invisible is the expression of the same Spirit. It is the Doer, the Doing, and the Deed; Seer, Seeing, and Seen; Knower, Knowing, and Known. Experiencing this truth is the purpose of life. Then we can enjoy an easeful, peaceful, and useful life. May all realize this and be happy and bring happiness to one and all. Om Shanti, Shanti, Shanti."

Sri Swami Satchidananda, spiritual head of the Integral Yoga Institutes and Ashrams

"Spirit is the light of life that shines in a child's eyes, a sunniness that refreshes the heart and hope of those who all too soon would allow it to dim."

Louis C. Scheinfeld, sports and entertainment firm owner

GLORIA STEINEM

Gloria Steinem's name has been synonymous with women's rights for more than 30 years. Her pioneer spirit helped to power an entire cultural movement. She was the founder of *Ms.*, the magazine that represented the women's rights movement, and is a devoted activist who traveled the country to bring everyone the message of feminism. To her, feminism is—and always was—the acceptance of men and women as equals.

Steinem sees herself more as someone who "responded to a need" than as someone who rushed off to follow a spiritual path.

Although the spirit of the movement—and Steinem's spirit—has changed over time, the women's movement is still going strong. "There is definitely still a women's movement," Steinem says. "I think the major change is that there is now a critical mass, and actually majority support for the idea of equality. There is now a critical mass of changed consciousness in the country—the women's movement does not feel as distant from the culture as it used to. And it is much more diverse.

"I think that at first the movement was very directed toward economic rights, the right to be safe from violence, and many very immediate bread-and-butter issues. We have grown to realize and to be able to explore more spiritual issues, too. To understand that if we do not do that, we will forever be consigned, in moments of sorrow or ritual, to religions that dishonor women. We have to make an alternative that honors women and all living things."

Steinem appreciates the diversity offered by the feminist spirituality movement, launched about 25 years ago. "I think that is a great help—showing not that God is only present in a female form, but that it's not only present in a male form either. God is present in all living things. It says there is an essence of God in all living things, not just human beings. It is just spirituality."

There have been times when Spirit seems to have spoken to her, she recalls. "I think in my early 50s, when I got burned out—for the umpteenth time—I really kind of hit bottom. I began to stop and consider more, which is when I wrote *Revolution from Within*. I was so exhausted from activism that I couldn't continue to act. I began to realize that I was out of balance. Your internal life is not *more* important than the external, but it is not less important either. And I had been totally externalized." It was around this time that she discovered she had breast cancer, which she heeded as a call to slow down and smell the flowers.

In the last decade or so, she has begun to believe that she may be on some sort of spiritual path after all. Growing older, especially, has renewed her Spirit. "Each thing has its own season. It feels a little odd at first, but the greatest reward of being over 60 is that the feminine role is over. Especially in this culture, but also in many cultures, the feminine role extends from fertility to the end of childbearing. After that, there's not much use for women. So in a way it's like being eight or nine again when you were climbing trees and saying 'I know what I want, I know what I think.' Only now you have your own apartment and a little money. It's like a whole new country."

What is Spirit? "There is an essence of the divine in all living things. And each person is literally a microcosm of the universe. Each person has a unique self, an individual self, that could never happen again. So you begin to trust an inner voice. It is not a straight line—not, 'first you do this and then you do that.' You keep on doing similar things over and over. It's a spiral, I think. It's not either/or, it's both/and. And that is Spirit."

"I believe that explaining what Spirit is, and, for that matter, explaining the importance of great music, is indefinable, in a way, because it has to do with feelings and inner feelings. Feelings are always very difficult to verbalize. In fact, in some ways, they are not to be verbalized—they are to be felt. When I think about Spirit, I think of a number of words: *love, uplifting, touching, otherworldly, religious, moving, depth,* and *emotion.* It is really about who we are and how we relate to life, how we question life, and how we try to understand it.

"It is the ability to be touched by other human beings, by great art, poetry, literature, and great music. It is our individual hope that as spiritual people we can make a contribution to society, to our families, and to our communities."

Gerard Schwarz, music director of the Seattle Symphony

Peter Max "Heart: Tropical #1" 1992, 36″ x 36″, acrylic-silkscreen on canvas

"Spirit is a metaphor
for the very phenomenon of evolution"

Jonas Salk

"Spirit is that warmth inside us that feeds our soul and makes our lives worth living. We are cold and lifeless without it. I feel our spiritual work is to be able to see that light within ourselves and others and live our lives trusting that light. A spiritual commitment to focus on God in every situation is what will bring us inner peace and Spirit."

Lonna Shuttlesworth, president of a distribution company

"What is Spirit? It is ineffable. One can only say what it is not. What is shared in this book should make that clear."

Bernie S. Siegel, M.D., retired surgeon; author of *Prescriptions for Living*

"Spirit is the essence of being. It is the life force of the mind and body, the animator of intellect. It is the Divine that moves through us, as us. Spirit is the All That Is, the simplicity of a single cell, and the mystery of a quark. It is the splendor of the rainbow and the grace of appreciation. It is the tenderness of singular touch and the collective comfort that being alone brings to meditation and creative thought. Spirit is full and empty. It is endless. It is forever. It is the cohesive force that holds the universe together. SPIRIT IS LOVE."

Rolland G. Smith, Emmy Award–winning broadcast journalist

"Recently, I was in the emergency room and I noticed a patient lying on a gurney. I asked the nurses who he was. I was told that I didn't need to see him, that he was a drunk punched in the face by a friend. I walked over to the man, feeling drawn to him, and I tried to arouse him. He was in a deep coma. A CAT scan was done and I took him to surgery immediately after the scan and removed shattered pieces of skull and a large blood clot strangling the normal brain. The man made a full recovery, and his life has changed forever. God and Spirit worked through me to give this man life. Today this man is a productive member of society. These situations occur frequently in my life. This was not the first time, and I know it will not be the last. I see the invisible. I have faith. This is Spirit! Vision is the ability to see what is not and to know it will be."

Clifford Solomon, M.D., FACS, surgeon who asks
Spirit to assist him during each operation

"Spirit is a magical essence, never seen but always felt. Spirit, when harnessed and directed, can affect not only the individual directly, but the world! Spirit is the embodiment and enhancement of our qualities, which when nurtured will deepen and have an intensifying effect on all of our natural capabilities. Spirit can be diverted and used as magical energy wherever and whenever it is needed most. Spirit is as unique and impossible to duplicate as a fingerprint or snowflake: no two are exactly the same. Spirit defines our spiritual, mental, and emotional capacities."

Theodore C. Solomon, businessman

"Spirit is the real person who inhabits the body that everyone recognizes as you. Your Spirit is the 'part' of you that will live on eternally. It is our Spirit that makes direct contact with God, who is Spirit."

Larry Speicher, pastor

"Spirit is the harmonic balance of our three selves—emotional, physical, and intellectual. This balance produces what are known as spirituality and well-being. When one self dominates and the balance is thrown off, there is a feeling of unease and turmoil. Because the balance is different for each person, much of life is understanding the balance and seeking to maintain it. This is why self-awareness is so linked to spirituality. Religion often provides frameworks that are useful in understanding this balance."

Quinn Spitzer, CEO of one of the top management consulting companies in the world

"Spirit connects mind, body, soul, and environment. Spirit lives in all things, stones to stars, water to wind. The Spirit of one may impact the Spirit of all found in its environment. Only through the understanding of the visible and invisible may one consciously alter the level of Spirit, and the awareness of such. My spirit existed long before this body, and shall go on long past this physical world. Spirit is what grants hope. May Peace Prevail."

Douglas Spotted Eagle, Native American flutist; promoter of world peace

"Spirit is the essential drive within an individual that influences that person to act."

Richard A. Sprague, attorney and law-firm owner

"Spirit is the force that compels one to continue striving forward when all logic fails to provide a reason to do so."

David Standig, telecommunications marketing executive

SIR JOHN TEMPLETON

Just to look at Sir John Templeton's face is to see the essence of Spirit. At 85, he beams with youthfulness and light. It could be nothing short of Spirit guiding his unique work in the world. The John Templeton Foundation supports extraordinary research with the aim of exploring and showing the link between science and Spirit. To put it more succinctly, he believes that science can prove the existence of God, and he is willing to invest millions based on that belief.

An investment manager for more than a half-century, Sir John has always been way ahead of his time. His investment philosophy took him to far-flung corners of the globe, and he made his fortune with The Templeton Fund, a mutual fund enterprise that went where no one else was going—often picking the least-popular stocks in unpopular markets—and won. It helped foot the bill for many spiritual expeditions as well.

The Tennessee-born Sir John—knighted by Queen Elizabeth in 1987—no longer manages The Templeton Fund. He is now completely engaged in The Templeton Foundation and his quest to bring as much spiritual knowledge and know-how to this planet as possible. Each year since 1973, he has awarded The Templeton Prize for Progress in Religion to a living individual who has shown extraordinary originality advancing the world's understanding of God or spirituality. The prize carries a $1 million award. His foundation funds "A Campaign for Forgiveness Research," an unprecedented scientific study exploring the unique role of forgiveness in healing individuals, families, communities, and nations. He sponsors symposiums such as *The Science of Forgiveness, The Science of Optimism and Hope, The Science of Wisdom and the Laws of Life,* and *Neuroscience and the Human Spirit.* He is committed to bringing society closer to a truer understanding of the bigger picture.

As Sir John sees it, science, medicine, and even religion have God in a box; he aims to open the lid and see what else is inside there. "My grandfather was a doctor, and a good one," Templeton says. "And three of my children are doctors. I can tell you my children know far more than my grandfather ever knew about the human body. But they know nothing more about the soul."

Sir John's spiritual awakening occurred over time. He survived many difficulties: having to put himself through Yale when his father could no longer afford it, watching his young wife die in a road accident, raising three young children on his own and having very little money to do it, the loss of his second wife to cancer. "It made me grow," he says.

There was no one single moment when Spirit spoke to him and guided him to leave his investment management business and put all his profits into the investigation of God and Spirit. "Gradually, little by little, I developed the idea that our life on Earth is very brief. And we ought to find out why we are here. What is the purpose of our life? What is the purpose of all of humanity? If we are going to have a short time, what should we do day by day? Should we use every second in order to do more good, not only to grow ourselves but to help other

Peter Max "Angel with Heart, Version III, #3" 1995, 20″ x 16″, acrylic on canvas

"Spirit is the essence and consciousness of one's soul— dark and enlightened. Both extremes are vital and should be left to flourish unrestricted. For in that journey discoveries are made"

Andy Garcia

people to grow? As Kipling said, 'If you can fill each unforgiving minute with 60 seconds worth of distance run, the earth is yours and all that's in it. And what's more, you will be a man, my son.' So that's my attitude toward learning spiritual thinking."

What is Spirit? "I would say it is humility," Sir John says. "It is a feeling that no human being has understood even one percent of the totality of spiritual information. And, therefore, we should be enthusiastic to try to discover it."

◇ ◇

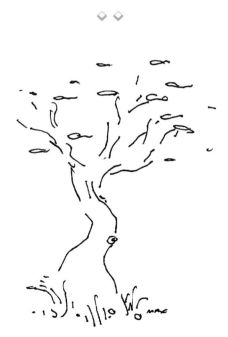

"I interpret the word *Spirit* to mean the will to act virtuously and to do good whenever possible, to rise above your own selfish interests. I think this is inherent in human nature and is what the Judeo-Christian ethic is all about; but more importantly, I think Spirit is living a virtuous life, doing the right thing, being decent to other people, trying to make a difference.

"It has been my experience that a positive Spirit, or will, that causes you to do things when every instinct says 'do not,' inures to one's benefit and makes you grow in an ethical and virtuous manner, giving you strength to go on when times become very difficult. Spirit is positive energy that one receives from living a decent and useful life."

Saul P. Steinberg, CEO of Reliance Group Holdings, Inc.

"Soul, consciousness, psyche, it is all the same. Spirit is the true identification of the human being …that inner core, the life force that is immortal. It sits behind the eyes and it is the master of the sense organs. The original and natural state of the Spirit is peace, love, purity, happiness, and power. Our Spirit belongs to the Supreme Spirit. When this ultimate connection is made then begins the return to Excellence."

Gita Stevenson, social worker

E. Fuller Torrey

E. Fuller Torrey, a psychiatrist who has dedicated 30 years of his life to understanding and helping patients combat severe mental illness, sees Spirit as the ability to put oneself in another's shoes and understand their pain. Describing himself as an atheist, Torrey feels Spirit is a demonstration of compassion in action.

He has authored 15 books, ranging from *Witch Doctors and Psychiatrists* to *Out of the Shadows: Confronting America's Mental Illness Crisis*. Today, as executive director of the Stanley Foundation Research Programs in Bethesda, Maryland, he is spearheading the foundation's humanitarian efforts in poverty-stricken Ethiopia. His work involves reaching out to young psychiatrists, local hospital staff, and nurses to support their efforts to help patients with severe psychiatric disabilities such as schizophrenia and manic depression. He delivers the assistance in the form of funds that he administers through the foundation, as well as hands-on training of local doctors who are striving to make a difference. This continues a crusade he began as a young doctor.

"I was a Peace Corps physician in Ethiopia from 1964 to 1966," says Torrey. "With a change in government in 1991, it became possible to get something done there." Even so, he notes, the support system for psychiatric cases in Ethiopia is dismal. On a recent trip, he visited a regional hospital where a single psychiatric nurse was the only psychiatric resource for more than two million people.

"This work, helping these medical professionals, is very gratifying because, when you start at the bottom, almost anything you do is going to improve things," he says. "Some of the Ethiopian doctors that have been trained in psychiatry elect not to go back. They are kind of taking in their $140,000 a year and living very well. The ones who have gone back to Ethiopia are working for $10,000 a year or less. They are very committed to making something happen in their country; therefore, they are a very nice group to work with."

What is Spirit to a man who does not rely on a God, yet who reaches out to others with great compassion, commitment, and soul? "Spirit can be interpreted very, very broadly in many different contexts—from a purely religious context, to the spirit you have when you go to a New York Yankees baseball game," he says. "My own motivation is not religious. I am a devout atheist, if you like. I recognize the need for some kind of inclusion in the universe, and certainly a very strong need to believe that there is something beyond death. I certainly would allow and encourage everyone to work out their spiritual needs in whatever way satisfies them, but I personally do not believe that myself.

"So my guess is that one of the important dimensions to Spirit is this presumably inborn ability to put yourself in other people's positions. And as much as you are able to put yourself in other people's positions, you are much more likely, I think, to act in a more altruistic spirit and try to help them. Some people have a great ability to put themselves in other people's positions and feel those people's pain. I don't think you can define spirit in a rather narrow sense, of irrational thought or something like that—you just have to take it on faith."

"Spirit is an energy. It is thinking with the mind but living with the heart. For it is life. It is my existence, my consciousness. We all have Spirit, every living being. It may be called your nature or your destiny, but it cannot be chained. It guides. You can develop it or let it stand, for it is free."

Bruce Strome, field coordinator of The Mystical Arts of Tibet

"You are Spirit. You are not a human having a spiritual experience. You are not Spirit having a human experience! You are only Spirit having a spiritual experience!"

Prema Baba Swamiji, spiritual leader

DONALD TRUMP

Most people do not think of Donald Trump and Spirit in the same breath. Even he says that he does not see Spirit as an unseen force connecting him to all living things. "I don't necessarily think it connects me to everything," he says. "And I do not go around thinking that all the time. There are people who maybe do, but I think that, ultimately, God is what it's all about."

Celebrity is Trump's middle name, and mega-million-dollar deals are his claim to fame. Yet he has a perspective on Spirit and spirituality that he rarely shows the world.

"I think Spirit and spirituality can be related but can also be different," Trump says. "I view spirituality differently from how I view the word *Spirit*. I believe strongly there is a God, and in terms of success, in terms of business, without the spirituality, you don't have much. But *spirit* is more a word of vigor, vim, and enthusiasm. *Spiritual* is a more Godly word.

"My energy level is one of the reasons I am able to make deals that other people cannot make, and I think that is related to Spirit. When it comes to the creation of things, and sometimes the creation of money, you often get there by your spirit or by enthusiasm.

"We're on this planet 60 or 80 years, which is just a speck of time relative to the age of the planet, the world, the universe. There has to be something more than our 70-year journey. We have to either be rewarded or demoted for who we have been and how we have treated life. Ultimately, we are all accountable to God."

What is Spirit? "Spirit is enthusiasm. If you do not have enthusiasm, you cannot be. The people I have found to be most successful are not necessarily the smartest people, but the people with the most spirit and enthusiasm. Without Spirit, you are nothing."

"Spirit is an energy force that engages us in self-inspiration. It is what makes us unique. It is why we reach for the stars and go beyond what is tangible. It is expressed through our conflict, our motivation, our creativity, our humor, our sadness, our love, and our feelings of connectedness. Spirit lives within us, and yet we also aspire to touch a Spirit that seems to live outside ourselves. It is a force that we try to reach, to emulate or reason with (for some believe it judges us), and make peace with, as well."

Janet Swartz, teacher, executive sales representative

"Spirit is the only real salvation of our soul, which is the flower in God's garden, and Spirit is the custodian."

Renato Taverna, maître'd

"Spirit is the indomitable will that keeps us going when situations look hopeless. Spirit is our soul, our conscience… the very essence of man."

Sandy Taxin, owner of The Original Bookbinders Restaurant in Philadelphia

"Spirit carries on when the body cannot, without physical and emotional limitation. Spirit is the hand that guides the tool, the pure essence of life."

Rachel Taylor, marketing director of the international shoe company Charles David

"Spirit is the innermost quality of a being. It is that part of us that is unstained, the primordial beauty from which we derive every inspiration, an inborn reservoir from which we can draw every jewel of excellence, the source of universal love and compassion, the clear radiance from which wisdom is born. When we connect with it, we connect with the whole universe. When we lose sight of it, we wander astray. A mere glimpse of it transforms our perspective on all that exists."

Geshe Lobsang Tenzin, director of the Deprung Loseling Monastery in North America

"Spirit represents the heart-essence of all things higher than self and personality, the energy flow that encompasses the soul's journey.

"In its truest and magical sense, Spirit is the pure and honest feelings from that part of a person that you cannot feel or touch, but is the best part of you, resonating to the world.

"Spirit, along with mind and body, is who we are."

Dorothy Thau, parapsychologist, holistic health counselor

ROSHUMBA WILLIAMS

Supermodel Roshumba Williams' face has blessed the covers of the *Sports Illustrated* swimsuit edition, *Vogue, Harpers Bazaar, Elle,* and *Allure.* She has graced the runway for Versace, Dior, St. Laurent, Oldham, and Armani. She's on television—from fashion segments to a recurring role in *Mortal Kombat*—and in the movies, appearing in Woody Allen's *Celebrity.*

Roshumba says she is on a mission to bring Spirit to modeling and feels her success is related to a beauty within. "My soul led me to modeling," she says. "I remember when I was 16, looking at a fashion magazine, something just snapped inside of me and said, *This is what I want to do.* To this day, 11 years later, I still don't believe I should be doing anything other than this. My mission has something to do with me being looked at as a beauty in the public eye; but it took some time for me to understand that meant an inner beauty."

In the early '90s, Spirit offered Roshumba a wake-up call that she'd slipped off her spiritual path. As her cab pulled up in front of her apartment, she got into an argument with the driver. "I said, 'You stupid man, you dummy, you idiot,'" she recalls. "I threw the money at him, got out of the cab, and slammed the door. After that fight, a voice came into my head and said, *You need to go away and find yourself.*"

The fight reflected the conflict between desiring success and all the privileges, and hungering for spiritual connection. She wanted both.

She headed for a stay at an ashram, a spiritual sanctuary in the Hindu tradition, and began practicing yoga for the spiritual benefits. She got in touch with her soul. It helped her step onto the path she now walks with great devotion. "Now I study formally about Spirit," she says. Explorations have also led Roshumba to shamanic and Japanese spirituality.

"We're coming out of a material-first civilization," she says. "The death of that civilization is giving birth to the Spirit-first civilization, which is based on placing the higher power—the creator of heaven and earth, Mother Nature, peace, love, happiness, harmony, light, humility, gratitude—before greed, lust, selfishness, and destruction. That's why we've reached the point where everybody is basically having to face their demons. We have to structure our lives to put Spirit first."

She's very conscious of the fact that those of us who aren't models are challenged by the way models are used to portray beauty in this culture. She says her mission is to show that beauty is an inside job. Although her outer shell draws attention, she feels that what's most important is the sparkle, joy, and spirit that she radiates from within—and that we all radiate from within.

"For so long it has been about that perfect stick figure," she says. "But oftentimes, that stick-figure beauty is in pain. Truth is, for every human being, that pain wont go away with a tube of lipstick. The only way to deal with that pain is to face those demons. Make peace with them. And therefore make peace with yourself. Then you can become beautiful."

What is Spirit? "Spirit for me is the life force. It's the energetic force that gives life. It's the energetic force that allows you to experience life, both good and bad. And it's the energetic force that takes life."

"Spirit is the limitless fuel that sustains happy people."

Jerome S. Tilis, retired marketing vice president

"Spirit is the inner essence—the true being—that which you truly are, once all the worldly possessions and physical being is removed. Spirit is self—the true power of inner being."

Mel Tonkon, M.D., physician, researcher, clinical professor of medicine

"Spirit is the context of everything/nothing that enables its students to align themselves inwardly with their Soul's intent and, from that place, to create with God as their partner.

"Spirit is no longer in time; it is through time. Spirit is eternal nowness, where the Soul replaces the personality as the center of consciousness, intention, and energy. The spiritual promise is then experienced as an ongoing, living reality that one chooses into each day."

Linda Noble Topf, M.A., minister, author, artist, inspirational speaker

◇

"I think we all have Spirit inside us. But I think Spirit comes from other people, too. It's the ability to find that energy in someone else, someone who helps you when you need the strength of spirit to overcome something. It happens to all of us on every level. Spirit is an emotion, and a place within us that has to be nurtured. It can be nurtured by somebody you believe in—a coach, an uncle, a sister, a mother, a father. Someone who can make you believe that you are capable of something. But it's got to be brought out somehow. Whether you turn to a friend, a priest, a rabbi, a deity, the spirit of God that is within you, or wherever you perceive Spirit to be—they ignite the Spirit in you.

"If you have Spirit, you can go on; you can overcome certain things by this inner energy and power and feeling. It makes you feel that you have an opportunity, a chance, a hope, a dream, an expectation, a relationship. You have to have Spirit to do practically anything in life. I have a lot of Spirit because I have a wonderful family and I am able to see that. I think you feel Spirit. And I do believe that your spirit goes on. I think there is a 'spiritual world.' Spirit is a big force. Tremendous."

Robert Wagner, TV and movie actor

❖

"Spirit is nonmanifested vibration. Spirit exists in a pure vacuum state and desires to become universal matter. Spirit is potentially conscious. We in our spiritual quests yearn to free our Spirit, and its bounded emanation called soul, from the traps of the material world. Spirit must always return to its nonmaterial state. Spirit is truly the domain where we merge with our universality."

Gailyn Waldron, CEO of an Aspen-based company
that develops socially conscious projects

"Spirit is the essence of all living things. Without Spirit, life would cease to exist. The drive and will to live, love, create, and reproduce would be no more. One could say our universe, our planet, and all living things throughout creation are Spirit."

Benny Ward, geologist and artist

"To me, Spirit is the vital essence of a person's powerful and refined desire, action, and reason. It is life as well as the embodiment of personality. To put it simply, Spirit is the enjoyment of life—the enjoyment of ourselves and friends, the admiration of the beauty of nature, the contentment we get from entertainment through the arts, the satisfaction gained from the food we eat, the enjoyment of home and family, and the celebration of everything that life offers."

Lanny Ward, musician, model, entrepreneur, teacher

JoHN WiNdwAlkER

"I think that Spirit is really the only reason that I got through my childhood," says clairvoyant and medical intuitive John Windwalker. "Spirit is the indescribable glue that has kept everything together for me. Even though I could not see it, I always knew it was there."

Windwalker is a sought-after practitioner and teacher with a home base in Princeton, New Jersey; he has been in spiritual service for 15 years, helping people to heal and awaken to their own intuition. His own awakening to Spirit occurred at a young age and with little fanfare, yet the life events that shaped his ongoing relationship with Spirit challenged him at every stage.

He described his family life as, on a good day, "totally, incredibly dysfunctional." As a child, he says, his dad was hot-tempered and physically abusive, and his mom was emotionally unbalanced. She had a nervous collapse when he was eight; he didn't see her for what seemed an eternity to an eight-year-old child. "It was really rough," he says. "There were three things that got me through: number one was music, two was sports, and three was what I would call quiet time because it was really meditation. I started meditating when I was about five."

The saving grace of being a child in that house was his brother, Gary. "My brother was very clairvoyant with me, and we thought everybody was, so we never really talked about it." They bonded as brothers and soul friends. Then tragedy struck. When Gary was 19, a drunk driver hit and killed him. Windwalker—devastated by the loss—turned to Spirit to try to understand, cope, and penetrate the veil that divided his world from Gary's.

Life delivered opportunities for Windwalker to follow Spirit's lead. Strong guidance led him to leave his home and practice in San Francisco and come East. "I had been visiting my mother, grandmother, and brother in New York for the first time in five years, and on the way home from the airport I heard a very clear, distinct voice say, 'There is nothing for you here. It is time for you to go.'" He meditated on it for three days, and that is when the call came in: An invitation to join a healing center in Princeton.

"My life is about getting to identify with the soul in me," he explains. "That is kind of what I teach—to trust that. And that is where I turn. In most cases, the path is understanding that everything is possible; that it is really 'seek and ye shall find,' or 'ask and ye shall receive.' It's true. But the greatest way to get anything is to have a grateful heart—simple gratefulness. We have so much spiritual help it is incredible. We feel so lonely and we despair so much, but there is so much help. In some cases, our helpers do not have bodies. But that doesn't mean they do not help us. They are unbelievable. The immensity of love in these incredible masters is indescribable, and that is really what heaven is. And heaven is in everybody. You can see it. Heaven is really in every single kind act."

What is Spirit? "I think many people want to label it in some way, and it is nothing that can be labeled," he surmises. "Spirit is non-beginning, non-ending love. I guess it would be called internal and everlasting—it really is all there is. It is joy and happiness. Spirit is really doing what we love and loving what we do in the highest sense, which is always toward love."

◇ ◇

"Spirit is a guiding force, known in those quiet moments when we allow ourselves to hear our innermost whispers. It is our internal compass, pointing to what is uniquely right for us. It is always there. Yet, we often silence the whispers of Spirit, finding comfort instead in the familiar, the expected, the easy. When these murmurings yank at our soul, Spirit is calling for our attention, endeavoring to help navigate our way.

"If we all listen to Spirit, imagine what we might become."

Petrina Fisher Wells, M.F.T, founder of the ADD Institute and Treatment Center

"For me, Spirit exists in the space between these words, in my connection with other beings, in the intimacy of family and friends, and in the expression of my personal purpose for living. Spirit acts to end separation, to facilitate healing, and to bring us together. Spirit is the purest expression of loving energy, which creates both the familiar known and the magical unknown."

Robert White, author; widely considered the founder of the personal growth movement

◇

"From a very young age, my family taught me that in order to be a great person, one must be rich in Spirit. In my personal quest to be rich in Spirit, I realized that Spirit is how much one can love—loving God, family, nature, others, and life itself. The more one is able to love, the closer one is to a higher Spirit. In return, one becomes a person rich in Spirit."

Nessie M. Yara, artist and photographer

*Use this page to write down your thoughts after reading
the diverse ideas and insights about Spirit.*

WHAT IS SPIRIT?

Parting Thoughts

My initial idea was to create a gift book filled with profound quotes and beautiful artwork by Peter Max. It was a simple concept. As the process unfolded and I started asking people what Spirit is, and how they experienced Spirit in their lives, deep and profound truths came forward. I became enthralled listening to people share their magnificent definitions of Spirit, how it transformed their lives, and the process of reaching personal understanding. The stories made me laugh, cry, and reexamine my own beliefs. Each quote and story is filled with rich and significant information. It was obvious that the content of my book was greatly enhanced by these inspirational stories and by those who participated in this uplifting and magical adventure.

As I listened to people's insights and concepts about Spirit, my knowledge of Spirit evolved. It has been one of the most enjoyable and stimulating journeys of my life. It opened my heart and transformed my understanding of Spirit.

Tibetan monks and people from all walks of life started to "show up" in my life. We discussed how we could collaborate and make a difference in the world. I am still meeting fascinating people, and more doors are continually opening! I know we are all supposed to work together in Spirit.

I am connecting with people on a much deeper level, and I'm having incredibly deep conversations with acquaintances I barely knew. Remarkably, I am discovering and creating deeper and more meaningful relationships with friends. I am relating to them on a more authentic level, and in some instances, I am getting to know their spiritual side.

It has been a journey of "evolution in action," which reminds me of the experience I had with Albert, my next-door neighbor. He was dying of a brain tumor. He called me one day and said, "Lexie, you are one of the most spiritual people I know."

I visited Albert and had long conversations with him every few weeks. We did everything from Reiki energy work to affirmations. I massaged his feet while we talked about life and death. We lit candles. We prayed. I sat and read him books and shared my own spiritual beliefs. He talked about his fear of death. We talked about our real purpose in life and created an affirmation that helped him find his own inner peace.

During this period, he evolved into one of the most spiritual human beings I have ever known. In the beginning, it appeared that I was helping him, but in reality he was helping me. My encounter with Albert was one of the most profound experiences of my life. He allowed me to get close to him at a time when he was crossing over. It was such an honor and a great privilege to experience him on such a sacred level. He allowed himself to be vulnerable with me. Words can't describe that awesome trust.

Near the end, he could barely walk to go to the bathroom. As he deteriorated, I no longer saw his physical body. Our affinity became that of an ethereal relationship. Through this deep connection with him, I experienced an inherent and intense connection with Spirit.

I went to see him a few weeks before he died. He asked me to give him a hug. So I did. Then he told me, "I just want you to know that I love you more than you will ever know." That was the last time I ever spoke with Albert.

When Albert was physically here, I felt his appreciation and his humor. Nevertheless, I still experience his laughter, appreciation, and love through Spirit. Albert touched hundreds of people's lives, as he did mine. His Spirit lives on through all of us who were so blessed to experience his love.

After Albert's death, I knew I wanted to work on a deeper, more spiritual level with people. I started to volunteer even more, and gave lectures at high schools; I became an ordained minister. And I started to write a book about Spirit. I now understand that everything I have done in my life thus far has prepared me for where I am today.

The intention behind this book is to serve. Spirit has guided me. As I look back over the past two years when it all started, there has been a perfect plan in place. Personally, I believe Spirit lives in each of us. Everyone, without exception, is a manifestation of God. We are all one—in our pain and our suffering, in our successes and our triumphs. Feeling connected to Spirit is what gives me inner peace. I believe God and Spirit guided me and brought me together with so many people to make this all happen.

I learned to find happiness from the steadfastness of my own heart, in my commitment to service, and in giving to others. Spirit is about all of us working together to make a difference, whether in this book, or solving community challenges. We need to use our abilities and resources to make a difference.

If we just take that first step, Spirit comes and supports us.

Ultimately, it's all about being open to Spirit. This journey has been about opening my heart. When we open our hearts to Spirit, we see the world with infinite, unbearable compassion. Spirit moves in miraculous ways when we stay open to the unlimited possibilities. When we do, peace, cooperation, love, forgiveness, and universal kindness become the norm.

This book was created as a vehicle for passing along some of those possibilities, perceptions, and feelings that people have so graciously shared. It was also created to serve and support others in rediscovering their own divinity. I sincerely hope that *What Is Spirit?* will remind us all of who we really are! We are meant to soar like eagles—and with Spirit, we *can!*

My Closing Blessing

I Pray That You Find Your Personal Path to Spirit

Self-discovery can unfold through many different paths.

True awareness comes about first and foremost by the desire to have it. Once you have a deep desire to discover who you are and what your purpose is, several paths will present themselves to you for consideration.

The choice is always yours. I encourage you to follow your heart and soul, and take the path that sings to you most.

Pick your personal yellow brick road and follow…follow…follow.

Indecisiveness impedes growth and slows down the journey. No true path of Spirit is carved in stone—Spirit wants us to be flexible, fluid, open to inspiration and transformation along the way. But Spirit can speak to us loud and clear when we have at least begun to focus our energies on *following a path*.

Spirit is what connects us to one another. It's about being open and allowing our higher selves to connect to the source of all that is. Spirit speaks to us in so many ways—it is the voice of God that comes to us through love, friendship, family, music, books, nature, animals, and all things.

Our job is simply to listen, open our hearts to hearing our own truth, and allow Spirit to move and direct us.

We are all beings of light, love, free will, and Spirit. When we choose to listen to the messages from the heart, we are so much closer to Spirit.

I lovingly pray that you choose to listen to the messages of your heart, that you find PEACE, LOVE, GRACE, and JOY, and that you lovingly hear the gentle guiding Spirit whispering in your ear!

I honor the divinity in you and the divinity in me. Stay on the path of Spirit and keep your heart open—and miracles will happen!

Lexie

Lexie with nine Tibetan Buddhist monks from the Drepung Loseling Monastery.
Photo: Tom Bollinger

LEXIE BROCKWAY POTAMKIN

Lexie Brockway Potamkin has traveled the globe, from India to Easter Island in her work as a human rights activist, counselor and minister. For the past five years she has utilized her travels to collect responses for *What is Spirit?*

Lexie came to her spiritual work with years of experience in the worlds of business, public relations, fashion and entertainment, she maintains a private practice in corporate management consulting. Her jobs have ranged from beauty queen (Miss World USA) to public relations executive, television talk show host, national spokesperson, to consumer advocate and lecturer. In 1990 she received her Masters in applied psychology from the University of Santa Monica.

In 1998, she became an ordained non-denominational minister.

She is currently president of Resources for Children's Health, a Philadelphia-based nonprofit organization that supports mothers and babies from high-risk groups; vice president of the International League for Human Rights in New York City; a trustee of The International House in Philadelphia; and in the pursuit of helping others and following her dreams.

To contact Lexie, please visit her website at: www.whatisspirit.com

PETER MAX

Peter Max is one of America's most popular artists, with paintings on exhibit in hundreds of museums and galleries worldwide. Max's opening at the Hermitage Museum in St. Petersburg, Russia, drew the largest opening night attendance for an artist in the history of the Soviet Union—over 14,500 people attended. Max has been commissioned to become the official artist for five Super Bowls, five Grammy Award shows, the U.S. Open, the World Cup soccer games, the 50th Anniversary of the United Nations, and other events too numerous to mention.

Peter Max had become an American pop hero in the late 1960s when his art captured the imagination of an entire generation. He had become to the art world what the Beatles were to music. Max's interpretation of the American flag, his annual tradition of painting the Statue of Liberty, and the fact that he has painted for the last five U.S. Presidents, has also earned him the reputation as "America's painter laureate."

Max's concerns for the environment and human and animal rights are as strong today as they have been throughout the years, often becoming the themes for his most popular posters. What people find the most appealing about Max's art are the vibrant colors and uplifting imagery, which capture the spirit of optimism that is reflected in his attitude toward life as well as art. A fascination with the exploration of space and new digital technology has been the driving force that has propelled Peter Max to become "the artist of the new millennium."

Index

Editor's Note: If an entry is italicized, it refers to a quote given by that individual. If the entry is bold, it refers to an inspirational tale about that individual written by the author, Lexie Brockway Potamkin.

Hay House Lifestyles Titles

Flip Books

101 Ways to Happiness, by Louise L. Hay
101 Ways to Health and Healing, by Louise L. Hay
101 Ways to Romance, by Barbara De Angelis, Ph.D.
101 Ways to Transform Your Life, by Dr. Wayne W. Dyer

Books

A Garden of Thoughts, by Louise L. Hay
Aromatherapy A–Z, by Connie Higley, Alan Higley, and Pat Leatham
Colors & Numbers, by Louise L. Hay
Constant Craving A–Z, by Doreen Virtue, Ph.D.
Dream Journal, by Leon Nacson
Healing with Herbs and Home Remedies A–Z, by Hanna Kroeger
Healing with the Angels Oracle Cards (booklet and card pack),
by Doreen Virtue, Ph.D.
Heal Your Body A–Z, by Louise L. Hay
Home Design with Feng Shui A–Z, by Terah Kathryn Collins
Homeopathy A–Z, by Dana Ullman, M.P.H.
Interpreting Dreams A–Z, by Leon Nacson
Natural Gardening A–Z, by Donald W. Trotter, Ph.D.
Weddings A–Z, by Deborah McCoy
What Color Is Your Personality? by Carol Ritberger, Ph.D.
What Is Spirit?, by Lexie Brockway Potamkin
You Can Heal Your Life, by Louise L. Hay
and
Power Thought Cards, by Louise L. Hay

All of the above titles may be ordered by calling
Hay House at the numbers on the last page.

We hope you enjoyed
this Hay House Lifestyles book.
If you would like to receive a free catalog
featuring additional
Hay House books and products,
or if you would like information about the
Hay Foundation, please contact:

Hay House, Inc.
P.O. Box 5100
Carlsbad, CA 92018-5100

(760) 431-7695 or (800) 654-5126
(760) 431-6948 (fax) or (800) 650-5115 (fax)

Please visit the Hay House Website at: www.hayhouse.com